the
BASKETBALL
BOOK *of*
WHY

(AND WHO, WHAT, WHEN, WHERE, AND HOW)

Also by the Author

1960: When the Pittsburgh Pirates Had Them All the Way

All The Moves I Had: A Football Life (with Raymond Berry)

America's Football Factory: Western Pennsylvania's Cradle of Quarterbacks from Johnny Unitas to Joe Montana

Baseball Dads

The Football Book of Why (and Who, What, Where, When, and How)

Name That Ballplayer

The New Book of Baseball Trivia

Remembering the Greatest Coaches and Games of the NFL Glory Years: An Inside Look at the Golden Age of Football

Remembering the Stars of the NFL Glory Years: An Inside Look at the Golden Age of Football

Stan the Man: The Life and Times of Stan Musial

Wits, Flakes and Clowns: The Colorful Characters of Baseball

You're the Basketball Ref: Mind-Boggling Questions to Test Your Basketball Knowledge

You're the Ref: 174 Scenarios to Test Your Football Knowledge

You're the Ump: Mind-Boggling Questions to Test Your Baseball Knowledge

the BASKETBALL BOOK of WHY

(AND WHO, WHAT, WHEN, WHERE, AND HOW)

THE ANSWERS TO QUESTIONS
YOU'VE ALWAYS WONDERED ABOUT HOOPS

WAYNE STEWART

Essex, Connecticut

An imprint of Globe Pequot, the trade division of
The Rowman & Littlefield Publishing Group, Inc.
4501 Forbes Blvd., Ste. 200
Lanham, MD 20706
www.rowman.com

Distributed by NATIONAL BOOK NETWORK

British Library Cataloguing in Publication Information available

Library of Congress Cataloging-in-Publication Data

Names: Stewart, Wayne, 1951- author.
Title: The basketball book of why (and who, what, when, where, and how) : the answers to
    questions you've always wondered about hoops / Wayne Stewart.
Description: Essex, Connecticut : Lyons Press, [2023] | Includes bibliographical references. |
    Summary: "How was basketball born? Why is the area in the paint and around the free throw
    circle known as the key? When did the NBA begin play? What team was arguably the worst
    NBA squad ever? Who was the highest drafted college player who never played a single
    game in the NBA? This book provides over 100 questions and detailed answers concerning
    the traditions, rules, and history of basketball. Organized by the sport's three eras-its birth
    through 1945, the NBA from 1946 through 1999, and the game today-it answers questions
    about the sport at all levels, from college games to the Olympics. A bonus chapter provides
    a Who, What, When, Where, Why and How of basketball-the perfect resource to settle
    arguments or to answer challenging trivia questions"— Provided by publisher.
Identifiers: LCCN 2023009215 (print) | LCCN 2023009216 (ebook) | ISBN
    9781493072767 (trade paperback) | ISBN 9781493072774 (epub)
Subjects: LCSH: Basketball—United States—History. | Basketball—United States—
    Miscellanea. | Basketball players—United States—History. | National Basketball
    Association—History.
Classification: LCC GV885.7 .S82 2023 (print) | LCC GV885.7 (ebook) | DDC
    796.3230973—dc23/20230621
LC record available at https://lccn.loc.gov/2023009215
LC ebook record available at https://lccn.loc.gov/2023009216

∞™ The paper used in this publication meets the minimum requirements of American
National Standard for Information Sciences—Permanence of Paper for Printed Library
Materials, ANSI/NISO Z39.48-1992.

To my family: wife Nancy, sons Sean and Scott, daughters-in-law Rachel and Katie, and my grandson Nathan.

Also to my father, O. J. Stewart, who taught me to love words and their power, and to my mother, Margaret (Jones) Stewart, who taught me to love to read.

Contents

Introduction

As was noted in *The Football Book of Why (and Who, What, When, Where, and How)*, a companion book to this one, any beginning journalist knows that every story they work on should, when applicable and relevant to the story, contain the answers to the questions readers are most curious about. These all-important questions are known as the five Ws and an H—who, what, when, where, why, and how.

To gain a full and rich understanding of the game of basketball, those questions are, of course, vital. Fans, even ardent ones, may know all of their favorite players' statistics and a great deal of the major records set by the game's greats, yet lack knowledge about some points involving basketball.

This book provides a slew of questions and in-depth answers mainly concerning the rules, records, history of the NCAA and the NBA (with an emphasis on professional basketball), and much more. From the early days of basketball to the globally popular game seen today, there's a good chance this book deals with questions every fan has pondered. Whether the topic is superstars or coaches, famous "firsts" or memorable moments, if a who, what, when, where, why, or how question is on your mind, this is the book for you.

The game of basketball has undertaken quite an evolutionary ride, one deserving of study. So sit back, relax, and get ready to be entertained, informed, and even surprised by the facts that follow.

CHAPTER ONE

THE ORIGINS AND EARLY DAYS OF AMERICAN BASKETBALL FROM ITS BIRTH THROUGH 1945

Modern fans often lack specific knowledge when it comes to the roots of basketball, its dusty background, and the names once familiar but now faded or forgotten. How did basketball get its start? What exactly are its roots? When and where did those roots first take hold?

It's hard to imagine how different today's game is from how it was as during its days of infancy. Today's above-the-rim style play and the game's laser-fast pace would have been as impossible for an early spectator of basketball to fathom as space exploration would have been to Christopher Columbus. This chapter will, in part, allow the reader to compare and contrast the sport from long ago to the way it has transformed to become the game it is today.

Now, should you happen to be one of those fans who isn't savvy about those early days, and you find such ancient history to be boring, then naturally you can either skim through this chapter or skip it entirely. However, be aware of this, if you skip the chapter, you'll miss out on some odd, fascinating, and entertaining items such as the following: What do peaches have to do with basketball's formative years? When did basketball get introduced as an Olympic event? Why do the Los Angeles Lakers have that nickname when the entire county of Los Angeles certainly has quite a few reservoirs but fewer than two dozen lakes?

WHEN WAS BASKETBALL BORN?

The sport was born way back in December 1891 when its first rules were published by the thirty-one-year-old Dr. James Naismith. That made this physical education professor and instructor at the International YMCA Training School in Springfield, Massachusetts, the father of basketball.

His purpose was to come up with an entertaining indoor activity his gym classes could take part in during the inclement days of the harsh New England winters. The students easily tired of the usual exercises such as calisthenics and marching. He not only achieved his goal, but he also created a game (one he called Basket Ball—which once had the proposed name of Naismith Ball) that grew into the international game we know today.

The *Official NBA Basketball Encyclopedia* states, "Naismith thought that elevating the goals would promote finesse and agility over the brute strength associated with football." Today there is an element of brute strength in the game to go along with sheer finesse.

At first basketball was played with a soccer ball. In 1894, soccer balls were replaced by a ball Naismith asked a company to produce for exclusive use in basketball—those were brown in color. Finally, in the late 1950s, a college coach named Tony Hinkle came up with the idea of making a ball that was more visible for everyone, and the orange basketball we know today was introduced.

WHO TOOK PART IN THE VERY FIRST BASKETBALL GAME?

In a 1939 radio interview, Naismith related the story. "I called the boys to the gym, divided them up into teams of nine, and gave them a little soccer ball . . . and I told them the idea was to throw the ball into the opposing team's peach basket. I blew the whistle, and the first game of basketball began."

Sounds simple enough, but the first game those two teams played turned into a melee. A *National Geographic* article quoted Naismith as saying, "The boys began tackling, kicking and punching in the crunches; they ended up in a free for all in the middle of the gym floor before I could pull them apart."

Naismith reeled off a list of injuries sustained in the fray, saying several players wound up with black eyes, one player got knocked out, and another had a dislocated shoulder. Like Dr. Frankenstein, he had to be thinking, *What have I created?* but when the students pleaded with him to allow them to have another game, he relented, but not before he devised additional rules to combat the turmoil.

WHAT WERE NAISMITH'S FIRST SET OF RULES?

The rules, some of which have remained on the books forever, evolved as Naismith came up with what is referred to as the "original 13 rules of basketball." The original list of the sacred rules was much sought after by collectors, selling for $4.3 million at a 2010 auction. The rules are:

1. The ball may be thrown in any direction with one or both hands.
2. The ball may be batted in any direction with one or both hands (never with the fist).
3. A player cannot run with the ball. The player must throw it from the spot on which he catches it, allowance to be made for a man who catches the ball running at a good speed if he tries to stop.
4. The ball must be held in or between the hands; the arms or body must not be used for holding it.
5. No shouldering, holding, pushing, tripping, or striking in any way the person of an opponent shall be allowed; the first infringement of this rule by any player shall count as a foul, the second shall disqualify him until the next goal is made, or, if there was evident intent to injure the person, for the whole of the game, no substitute allowed.
6. A foul is striking at the ball with the fist, violations of rules 3, 4, and such as described in rule 5.
7. If either side makes three consecutive fouls, it shall count as a goal for the opponents (consecutive means without the opponents in the meantime making a foul).

8. A goal shall be made when the ball is thrown or batted from the grounds into the basket and stays there, providing those defending the goal do no touch or disturb the goal. If the ball rests on the edges, and the opponent moves the basket, it shall count as a goal.

9. When the ball goes out of bounds, it shall be thrown into the field of play by the person first touching it. In case of dispute, the umpire shall throw it straight into the field. The thrower-in is allowed five seconds; if he holds it longer, it shall go to the opponent. If any side persists in delaying the game, the umpire shall call a foul on that side.

10. The umpire shall be the judge of the men and shall note the fouls and notify the referee when three consecutive fouls have been made. He shall have power to disqualify men according to rule 5.

11. The referee shall be the judge of the ball and shall decide when the ball is in play, in bounds, to which side it belongs, and shall keep the time. He shall decide when a goal has been made, and keep account of the goals with any other duties that are usually performed by a referee.

12. The time shall be two 15-minute halves, with five minutes' rest between.

13. The side making the most goals in that time shall be declared the winner. In the case of a draw, the game may, by agreement of the captains, be continued until another goal is made.

HOW WERE THE FIRST BASKETS DIFFERENT FROM THOSE USED TODAY?

The baskets originally used were, in fact, just that—peach baskets. Here's how that played out: Naismith originally planned on using two square boxes as targets for players' shots, so he asked a janitor to come up with those containers. However, the janitor returned with two peach baskets instead. Improvising, Naismith nailed the baskets to the railing of an elevated running track at the YMCA in Springfield, Massachusetts, with one on each side of the playing area. By chance, the railing was 10 feet off the ground.

Of course, the baskets had no opening in their bottom, which would allow the ball to fall back into play after each made basket. The solution was simple, but a bit tedious and certainly impractical in the long run. One person had to be stationed at each end of the balcony, waiting to pluck the ball out of the basket and return it to the players below. Soon the decision was made to make a relatively small hole in the bottom of the peach baskets, which helped a bit, but someone still had to use a dowel to poke the ball up and out of the basket after every bucket. Long ago, a jump ball took place after each made bucket.

Now, of course, a net dangles from a rim, and the ball can easily fall through the net, ready to be scooped up and put back into play.

WHEN DID THE FIRST OFFICIAL BASKETBALL GAME TAKE PLACE, ONE THAT WAS PLAYED IN FRONT OF SPECTATORS AS OPPOSED TO THE ONES HELD AMONG NAISMITH'S STUDENTS?

National Geographic stated that the first public game was in a YMCA gym on March 12, 1892, pitting instructors against students. A reported two hundred fans were in attendance to witness the students easily dispatch the teachers by a score of 5–1 with each bucket being worth one point.

Back then, players took to a court that was about half the size of a current NBA court. It would be about five more years before the concept of playing five on a side became the standard.

HOW LONG DID IT TAKE FOR THE GAME TO CATCH ON AND SPREAD THROUGHOUT THE NATION?

Not long at all—a matter of weeks. The word spread from school to school and YMCAs became the showcase for a rapidly growing number of games. The process was expedited when Naismith's rules were published in a college magazine sent to numerous YMCAs throughout the nation. High schools followed and, according to *National Geographic*, "by 1905, basketball was officially recognized as a permanent winter sport."

Furthermore, "In 1892, less than a year after Naismith created the sport, Smith College gymnastics instructor Senda Berenson introduced the game to women's athletics." While the identity of the two men's teams involved in the first intercollegiate hoop game is in dispute, the first such women's game occurred in 1896 when Stanford University and the University of California at Berkeley squared off.

That year also featured what is widely considered to be the first pro game, held in Trenton, New Jersey, when a team from that city rented a hall and charged admission. Each player wound up earning $15 on the night after splitting profits—each player, that is, except one. With one dollar left over after an even split, the team captain, Fred Cooper, was awarded the bonus, making him basketball's first "highest-paid player."

WHAT WAS THE FIRST LEAGUE OF PROFESSIONAL BASKETBALL PLAYERS?

That league was the National Basketball League (the NBL) formed in August 1898, and it was made up of six teams in the Philadelphia vicinity. The league expanded two months later to eighteen teams, but it lasted only a short time. It was dissolved after five years, but the league would be reintroduced in 1937 with an entirely new support system, with Goodyear, Firestone, and General Electric corporations as the league owners.

The 1937 version of the NBL began with thirteen teams. According to the website NBAHoopsOnline.com, "The league began rather informally. Scheduling was left to the discretion of each of the teams, as long as the team played at least ten games and four of them were on the road … Games consisted either of four ten-minute quarters or three fifteen-minute periods. The choice was made by the home team. Some of the teams were independent, while others were owned by companies that also found jobs for their players."

The NBL was made up of teams from unlikely places and strange-sounding names. The charter members of the NBL were the league's first champions, the Akron Goodyear Wingfoots; Dayton Metropolitans; Buffalo Bisons; Fort Wayne General Electrics; Oshkosh All-Stars; Akron Firestone Non-Skids; Cincinnati Comellos; Kankakee Gallagher Trojans; Indianapolis Kautskys; Pittsburgh Pirates; Whiting Ciesar All-Americans; Columbus Athletic Supply; and the Warren Penns.

Other teams joined the league later, including the Denver Nuggets, the Detroit Vagabond Kings, and another one called the Sheboygan Red Skins (it was a different era back then).

WHEN DID PEACH BASKETS GET REPLACED BY MORE MODERN EQUIPMENT?

Peach baskets were in use until 1906, when they were replaced by metal hoops and nets. Finally, the ball could pass unhindered through the bucket. Backboards were added at that time, too, and for a good reason. Fans who watched games from spots near the basket on the balcony would sometime interfere with shots, but they could no longer do that once backboards obstructing their movements came along. Adding backboards also meant players could attempt bank shots.

WHAT IS CONSIDERED THE FIRST TIME A PLAYER DUNKED A BALL IN A CONTEST?

The first dunk in an organized game took place in 1936 during an Olympic contest. A 6' 8" player named Joe Fortenberry is credited as having invented the dunk—and at first it was scorned by purists of the game.

Phog Allen, legendary coach at the University of Kansas, wrote about the shot in his 1937 book, *Better Basketball Technique, Tactics, Tales.* "Dunking does not display basketball skill—only height advantage," he scoffed. According to TheSportsRush.com, dunks still faced "widespread disapproval" in the decades of the 1950s and 1960s (though many fans dispute that claim as being too broad).

Bob Kurland, one of the earliest seven footers to play college ball, is credited as being the first player to dunk in a college game. That took place in 1944 during a 46–44 Oklahoma loss to Temple. The NCAA website quotes Kurland from an *Orlando Sentinel* interview as saying, "The ball happened to be under the basket. I got it up and stuffed it in. That started it, I guess. It was an unintentional accident. It wasn't planned, just a spontaneous play in Philadelphia." Kurland, who was out of Oklahoma State when it was known as Oklahoma A&M, led his team to back-to-back NCAA titles in 1945 and 1946, being named the tournament's Most Outstanding Player (MOP) both years. He was a three-time Consensus First Team All-American (1944–1946).

"Kurland's imposing size and skill at the rim helped prompt the NCAA to also add a rule against goaltending. From Oklahoma State's media guide: 'It is probable that Kurland had more to do with the rule against goaltending than any player since he was the chief target of the rule.'" Before goaltending was banned in 1944, he blocked seventeen shots in one game.

He was chosen by the St. Louis Bombers in the fourth round of the 1947 Draft, but never played at the pro level. He chose instead to play for an Amateur Athletic Union (AAU) team, the Phillips 66ers, which he guided to three championships over a six-year period beginning with the 1946–1947 season. Still eligible for Olympic play, having never played pro ball, he appeared in two Olympics in 1948 and 1952, each resulting in a gold medal even though he only averaged 9.3 and 9.9 points per game (ppg.) during those Olympics.

WHY IS THE PAINTED AREA AROUND THE FREE THROW CIRCLE KNOWN AS THE KEY?

When the NBA lane was only 6 feet wide but ballooned to a circle around the free throw line and on up to the "top of the key," that formation made the area resemble (sort of) a key—with a narrow lane leading up to a rounded circle, like the part of a key people hold. The technical definition of the key now is the part of the basketball court extending from the foul line to the endline. By that definition, the key is now rectangular in shape and not at all key-like.

WHEN DID THE SPORT BECOME AN OLYMPIC EVENT?

The International Olympic Committee saw fit to introduce basketball at the 1904 games, but first only as a demonstration event. It took until 1936 for it to become a medal event for men and forty more years before basketball became a women's medal event.

The United States dominated play in men's basketball for decades. That is, until a chaotic fiasco of a game took place at the 1972 Olympics. More on that later.

WHEN DID THE FIRST NCAA TOURNAMENT TAKE PLACE AND HOW WAS IT DIFFERENT FROM WHAT WE SEE NOWADAYS?

The first tourney took place in 1939 and the Final Four was held at Patten Gymnasium on the campus of Northwestern University. The capacity of that site was puny (around 4,500–5,000) compared to, say, the Superdome in New Orleans, which, in 2022, housed the Final Four in a facility with a capacity of around 74,000.

The 1939 National Collegiate Athletic Association (NCAA) Tournament had a field so small a team had to win only one game to advance to what is now known as the Final Four. That's right, there were just eight teams at the event, so while making it to the Final Four now is an honor, back then it was simply a first step toward a goal, and hardly a distant goal. The teams were chosen by regions and no automatic qualifiers existed back then.

Likewise, it took just three victories to win the title. The first NCAA championship squad was the University of Oregon, which earned wins over Texas in the West Regionals, against Oklahoma in the semifinals, and with a 46–33 victory over Ohio State. Two teams, the University of Oklahoma and Brown University, entered the tourney with just nineteen games played, while Oregon had completed a thirty-one-game season.

WHAT POSTSEASON COLLEGE BASKETBALL TOURNAMENT WAS THE MOST PRESTIGIOUS ONE—AT FIRST, THAT IS?

The National Invitation Tournament (NIT), originally held in Madison Square Garden, was *the* tournament, clearly more important than the NCAA tourney at first. It began in 1938 with a field of four teams, two from the East and one team each from the West and Midwest. So the NIT predates the NCAA's tourney by one year.

BigBlueHistory.net states that the NIT "was such a draw that the NCAA scheduled their tournament after the NIT in order to avoid competing directly with it. This allowed some schools the opportunity to compete in both tournaments, with City College of New York being the first and only school to win both titles in the same year in 1950. Kentucky won three NCAA titles (1948, 1949, and 1951) and one NIT title (1946) during the time period that both tournaments were considered prestigious."

As the 1950s rolled around, the NCAA gradually stripped the NIT of its importance by "making it mandatory for winners of the top-10 conferences to participate in the NCAA Tournament and not the NIT. In addition, the NCAA began to expand their field, first to 16 teams (from 8) and then to 22 teams. This further put a crimp on the NIT."

Now, with sixty-eight teams headed to the NCAA Tournament, the status of the NIT has been greatly reduced.

WHY WERE BASKETBALL PLAYERS ONCE CALLED "CAGERS"—WHAT DOES A CAGE HAVE TO DO WITH BASKETBALL?

The Trenton team, wearing "uniforms featuring long tights and velvet shorts," did play inside a wire cage (at first made of chicken wire and later made of steel mesh) which enclosed the court and protected the players from rowdy spectators and vice versa. Plus, any ball deflected off the cage remained in play, saving time.

There was a drawback, though. One star from that era, Barney Sedran, said that at times a player would get thrown up against the wire and come away with cuts. "The court was covered with blood," he said.

The *Official NBA Basketball Encyclopedia* states the game looked more like a football scrimmage than today's basketball, and players sported pads on their knees, elbows, and shins. "Since no padding had been designed for faces, broken noses were not uncommon." Fans sometimes punched players while others were content to merely jab hatpins "and lighted cigarettes through the cages at the players' legs. In tough Pennsylvania coal towns, miners favored nails, which they would heat with mining lamps and throw in the direction of the referee or the opposing free-throw shooter." Sometimes games were precariously held on floors that had been waxed heavily for an upcoming dance.

WHAT WAS THE FIRST LEAGUE TO BEGIN ON A TRULY NATIONAL BASIS, SIMILAR TO WHAT MAJOR LEAGUE BASEBALL HAD ALREADY ESTABLISHED?

The American Basketball League (ABL) opened its doors in 1925, organized by George Preston Marshall, who later owned the Washington Redskins; George Halas, who owned the Chicago Bears; and a department store magnate named Max Rosenblum, whose eponymous team out of Cleveland won the championship.

This league mandated players sign exclusive contracts to stop them from jumping from team to team as had often happened earlier. They also banned the use of cages, the two-handed dribble, which was in use by other professional teams, and required their venues to use backboards. Two other important rules were the three-second violation and disqualifying players who committed five personal fouls.

The sucker punch of the Great Depression led to the league's demise. Its final season was 1930–1931. One somewhat robust team from the ABL, the Celtics, resorted to barnstorming, and were satisfied given the hard times to play for a guaranteed $250, far from their previous highs of about $1,000 per game. They were reduced to travel not by trains but by cars, with their star center and future Hall of Famer Joe Lapchick having to handle driving duties—he was a cross between a basketball legend and a Ralph Kramden.

WHAT OTHER MAJOR BASKETBALL LEAGUE CAME ALONG NEXT?

The National Basketball League (NBL) was born in 1937. College ball was the focus of most basketball fans during the Depression, with Madison Square Garden being the game's mecca. The National Invitational Tournament (NIT) began in 1938, and the then-lesser-regarded NCAA Tournament followed the next year.

Cashing in on the popularity of the college game, the NBL figured that if they drafted the big stars out of college, they could form a profitable league. Companies such as Goodyear, Firestone, and General Electric fielded teams and offered jobs to entice college seniors to play for them.

One team called the Whiting Ciesar All-Americans out of Indiana signed three-time All-American John Wooden to a contract. He played for them while also continuing to coach a high school team.

One quirk of the league during its inaugural season was that the home team was given the right to decide if they would use the center jump after each bucket or not. The center jump was eliminated the following season in this eight-team league. The NBL helped change the game when, in 1939, they added a rule requiring a team to move the ball past the center court line in no more than 10 seconds.

CHAPTER TWO

THE NBA FROM 1946 THROUGH 1999

It's ironic that basketball is regarded as the only major sport to originate in the United States of America, albeit by Dr. Naismith, who was Canadian, yet the NBA held its very first game outside the United States.

This chapter traces basketball from what is considered by some to be the NBA's first official season, 1946, through the end of the twentieth century (the league would not go by the name of National Basketball Association until 1949). We'll look at the birth pangs and struggles of the league all the way through the dynasties and dynamic stars that made the sport into an international success.

WHEN DID THE NBA BEGIN PLAY?

Two leagues, the Basketball Association of America (BAA or BAOA), which began play in 1946, and the National Basketball League (NBL) merged in 1949 to form the NBA after these rival leagues had previously slugged it out to sign top players and emerge as *the* league.

Five active teams in the NBA have roots in the NBL: the Rochester Royals, now the Sacramento Kings; the Fort Wayne Zollner Pistons, who, of course, became the Detroit Pistons; the Syracuse Nationals, now the Philadelphia 76ers; the Buffalo Bisons/ Tri-Cities Blackhawks, who now play as the Atlanta Hawks; and the Minneapolis Lakers who moved to the West Coast to become the Los Angeles Lakers.

As late as the mid-1950s, half of the NBA teams were located in cities with populations below one million. In 1957, an exodus from small cities started with the Royals moving to Cincinnati and the Pistons being transplanted to Detroit.

By the way, the NBL broke the color barrier by signing Black players five years before Jackie Robinson first played Major League Baseball with the Brooklyn Dodgers in 1947.

THE NBL ASIDE, WHAT ACTIVE TEAMS WERE IN THE NBA DATING ALL THE WAY BACK TO 1946?

Three teams can make that claim. The Boston Celtics have been in the league that long and have stayed in the same city and used the same nickname for that entire length of time. Similarly, the New York Knickerbockers fit that same description, although no one nowadays calls them anything except the Knicks. In the meantime, the Golden State Warriors also go back to 1946. They began in the East as the Philadelphia Warriors, moved to the West Coast in 1962, becoming the San Francisco Warriors, and then took on the name Golden State Warriors in 1971.

A few other teams go way, way back, but not quite to 1946. Three teams joined the NBA in 1948, the Fort Wayne Pistons who moved to Detroit in 1957, the Minneapolis Lakers who became stationed in Los Angeles in 1960, and the Rochester Royals who have gone by four other names—the Cincinnati Royals (1957), the Kansas City–Omaha Kings (1972), the Kansas City Kings (1975), and the Sacramento Kings (1985).

Trivia sidenote: some current teams have nicknames that seem incongruous, but a look at the game's history clears matters up. For example, the city of Los Angeles is not exactly known for its lakes, but the Lakers' first hometown of Minneapolis is located in Minnesota, which is known as the "Land of 10,000 Lakes." It actually has 14,444 lakes that cover ten or more acres, but putting the "Land of 14,444 Lakes" on the state's license plates just doesn't look right.

One other example: jazz is hardly the genre of music most associated with Utah, but that franchise began in New Orleans, so history lessons do pay off. The Jazz franchise first opened for business in the 1974–1975 season, but it floundered there. It made the move to Salt Lake City before the 1979–1980 season began.

WHEN AND WHERE WAS THE FIRST NBA GAME PLAYED? ALSO, WHAT TEAMS OPPOSED EACH OTHER THAT DAY?

On November 1, 2021, the NBA celebrated the seventy-fifth anniversary of its first contest ever. That game was between the New York Knickerbockers and the Toronto Huskies. A New York newspaper headline proclaimed, "Eleven players will make up the roster of the Knickerbockers when the Madison Square Garden entrant leaves tomorrow night to open its Basketball Association of America campaign in Toronto." As touched upon, the American game has definite Canadian roots.

The NBA touched off a season-long tribute to its anniversary season with a matchup of the Knicks and the Toronto Raptors. The NBA considers the BAA to be part of the NBA, which began play in 1946 even though, as mentioned earlier, the name National Basketball Association wasn't officially used until 1949.

The first game drew 7,090 spectators to the Maple Leaf Gardens to see the Knicks win a tight one, 68–66. New York's Ossie Schectman scored the first points in the history of the NBA and wound up with 11, three behind teammate Leo Gottlieb, the winner's high scorer. The top scorer was Ed Sadowski with 18.

Years later, Schectman spoke about the play as a "a simple give and go." He added that Gottlieb, who recorded the NBA's first assist, "very rarely passed the ball. I used to kid him for a long time,

'Leo, that was the first and best and last pass you ever made in your career.'"

A newspaper ad placed by the Huskies to hype the game featured a picture of their big man, 6' 8" George Nostrand, and the words "Can You Top This," with an arrow pointing at the image of Nostrand. The promotional gimmick was simple: "Anyone Taller Than NOSTRAND 6 Ft. 8 Inches Will Be Admitted Free to OPENING Game." The ad listed ticket prices at $0.75, $1.25, $2.00, and, for the finest seats in the house, $2.50. Had this promotion been held nowadays, about 3,200 fans could have entered for free. Of course, that's based on the very improbable event that every US resident who stands above 6' 8" would be eager to travel to the Garden to cash in on the deal.

WHAT DID THE BOX SCORE FOR THAT FIRST GAME LOOK LIKE?

Unlike today's sources for in-depth information about games, old box scores covered just the bare minimum of data. Players' last names were listed with their positions and three statistical categories followed in columns G, F, and P. Fans could see how many field goals a player sank, how many free throws he hit, and his point total—that's it.

As the NBA website points out, "Now we receive a plethora of stats in real time, and detailed player-tracking data within an hour of the final buzzer that can tell us how far and how fast a player moved, how many times he dribbled the ball and how close he was defended on his shots."

The website also notes that the NBA had nothing but white players when the league began. Seventy-five years later for the anniversary game, "only one player (New York's Evan Fournier of France) in the starting lineups will not be Black." That contest served as a celebration as well as "a reminder of how far the game and the league has grown over the past 75 years."

As for the players' positions when the NBA began, men were considered to play LF for left forward, RF for right forward, LG for left guard, and RG for right guard. Naturally, one position, the center, has retained the simple C abbreviation from day one.

WHO IS CREDITED AS COMING UP WITH (OR POPULARIZING) THE FIRST ONE-HANDED JUMP SHOT, WHICH LED TO THE EVENTUAL DISAPPEARANCE OF THE TWO-HANDED SET SHOT?

Hank Luisetti came up with an off-the-dribble, jumping one-handed shot during his three years at Stanford where he averaged 16.1 ppg. On New Year's Day of 1938, he became the first NCAA player to hit for 50 in a game, doing so versus Duquesne. He stunned the crowd by putting up more than half of his team's 92 points that evening and helping Stanford win by 65 points. He left the school as the game's all-time leading scorer, and his 50-point outburst remains a school record.

Before Luisetti, players normally shot like this description from SportsHistoryNetwork.com, "You would put your feet fairly close together, bend at the knees, and launch the ball using both hands. It kind of looked like a chest pass toward the ceiling. You wanted a nice arc on the ball. And you would never, ever leave the floor. Your feet maintained contact with the court." That meant that normally a shooter had to be wide open before they would consider letting the ball fly.

Luisetti revolutionized the game, often scoring in the 30s in an era where teams might score around 40 points or so per game.

Now, the kicker is this—nobody can say he really invented the new style of shooting for a simple reason. Nobody knows who was the very first person to fool around with the one-handed jumper. SportsHistoryNetwork.com continues, "It would be like trying to figure out who first discovered fire."

Experts believe that when Luisetti unveiled his shot for the first time under a bright spotlight, in a game held at Madison Square Garden in 1936, the one-handed jumper really gained exposure. Attention paid to the shot quickly spread from what it had been receiving mainly out West, far away from the media capital. East Coast schools began to adopt the shot and it was obvious the jumper was here to stay.

Here's another kicker—many sources say Luisetti most certainly does not deserve credit for inventing the shot, asserting that Glenn Roberts is the true father of the jump shot, becoming a figurative father while still in high school. He led his Christopher Gist High School to two state titles and a 35–0 season in 1931. He went on to play in the old NBL for three seasons (3.6 ppg.).

Another name thrown into the ring of pioneers is Kenny Sailors, who said his discovery showed once again that necessity is the mother of invention because his first jumpers came about because he needed to get shots off against his older brother who stood about 10 inches taller. The problem with this claim is that it purports his jumper first took place in 1932, perhaps a full year after Roberts began employing the shot—and in a pickup game. Still, Sailors wound up as a star for the 1943 NCAA champion University of Wyoming. He was selected as the tournament's MOP. He lasted from 1947 to 1951 in the NBA, averaging 12.6 ppg.

Joe Fulks, aptly nicknamed "Jumpin' Joe," who led the BAA in scoring during its first season, is considered another early practitioner of today's jump shot. The future Hall of Fame power forward won the 1946–1947 scoring title by 6.4 points over the second-highest scorer, Bob Feerick. That margin stood as the largest one for fifteen seasons, and his 63 points in a game played before the use of the 24-second shot clock was a record that stood for a decade.

WHO WAS THE FIRST MAN EVER DRAFTED INTO THE NBA?

The first draft was called the 1947 BAA Draft, and Clifton McNeely was the number one selection that year. Although he stood just 5' 10", he was a forward out of Texas Wesleyan University. He was selected to play for a team known as the Pittsburgh Ironmen. The Texas native led the National Association of Intercollegiate Athletics (NAIA) in scoring in his senior year. Instead of playing for Pittsburgh, he chose to pursue a high-school coaching career in his home state. Perhaps that was a wise move as the Ironmen folded in 1947 after only one season.

WHO WAS ONE PARTICULARLY NOTABLE PLAYER FOR THE IRONMEN?

The Pittsburgh team had a 6' guard by the name of Press Maravich who hailed from nearby Aliquippa, Pennsylvania. His real first name was Petar, but his nickname came from his job selling the *Pittsburgh Press* on the streets of his hometown.

That steel town has produced an inordinate number of pro stars, especially football stars such as Hall of Fame tight end Mike Ditka, four-time All-Pro defensive back Darrelle Revis, a two-time All-Pro defensive back in Ty Law, and defensive lineman Sean Gilbert, who played in one Pro Bowl. In all, eleven NFL players have hailed from Aliquippa. Additionally, the town was the birthplace of Press's son Pete who would play his high school ball in North Carolina after his father took an assistant coaching job there for NC State.

Later, in 1966, Press became the head coach at Louisiana State University. The next season Press went about his recruiting chores and offered a scholarship to, of course, his son, reportedly saying, "If you don't sign this . . . don't ever come into my house again."

HOW GOOD WAS PISTOL PETE, AND HOW MUCH DID HE HELP HIS FATHER AND THE LSU PROGRAM?

Pete was as good as people thought he'd be (maybe better), but the answer to the second part of the question is debatable. Certainly the 6' 5" Maravich was a sensation at LSU, scoring and passing with the deadeye of a sniper while showing off his flashy moves. Some players are as mobile as a mannequin, but he was as fluid as mercury.

The NBA website states, "Maravich wasn't the first player to dribble behind his back or make a deft between-the-legs pass. But his playground moves, circus shots, and hotdog passes were considered outrageous during his era." Anyone wanting to see some of the fantastic things he could do with a basketball need only go to YouTube.

He had to carry the load at LSU, and in some ways he fit the definition of a basketball gunner, more than glad to put the ball up again and again. Over his three seasons as a Tiger, "Pistol Pete" took slightly more than half of his team's shots from the field. In his first season, he shot 53 percent of LSU's field goal attempts, but the team's field goal percentage was higher than his in each of his three LSU seasons. He once led the NBA in field goal attempts as well.

Of course, coaches want their stars to take a whole bunch of shots—teammates referred to Celtics Hall of Famer Kevin McHale as the Black Hole, because a pass to him in the low post was attracted to McHale by his strong gravitational pull, and the ball, once in his hands, was not coming back out. To be fair to Maravich, though, he was a shooting guard, but he still managed to hand out 5.4 apg. over his NBA career. Maravich, heavily counted upon, especially in college, to put the ball through the hoop, scored just over 48 percent of all the points the Tigers scored during his stay at Baton Rouge, Louisiana.

On the freshman squad (in the time when freshmen could not play at the varsity level), he averaged 43.6 ppg., gaining instant broad attention throughout the basketball world. He followed that up with averages of 43.8, 44.2, and an ungodly 44.5 ppg. He not only led the nation in scoring all three years, one season he hit for 50 or more points in ten of his team's thirty-two contests. As a senior, he set NCAA records with his 44.5 ppg. and for the most points ever scored in a season, 1,381.

Maravich also owns virtually every major career-scoring record in the annals of the NCAA: he racked up 3,667 points the way Ebenezer Scrooge piled up coins. His lifetime collegiate scoring average is 44.2 ppg. He attempted and made more field goals than anyone, and he owns the most career 50-point games ever with twenty-eight.

While he did carry the Tigers on his shoulders, the burden proved to be a bit too heavy. LSU could only manage records of 14–12 and 13–13 in his first two seasons. It wasn't until his senior year, when he was named College Player of the Year, that they posted a solid record at 22–10 and got an invitation to the NIT, where they won two contests before losing to Marquette.

Maravich's dribbling skills rivaled those of the best of the Harlem Globetrotters, and his dazzling passing prowess made fans gasp. He could shoot from anywhere, so he is among the many players from long ago who wish the three-point shot had been around for their careers. In Maravich's case, the rule was first put into play in the NBA during his final three seasons. Although the sampling is small, he did hit the long-range shots at a .667 pace.

Unlike his son, Press lasted just one year at the pro level with the Ironmen, shooting a paltry .272 from the field and averaging a mere 4.6 ppg. By way of contrast, Pete's lifetime field goal percentage stood at .441, and he once led the NBA in points scored.

He also once put 68 points up even with defensive whiz Walt Frazier trying to stop, or at least slow him down. The Hall of Famer averaged 23.6 ppg. over his eleven NBA seasons with a personal high of 31.1 ppg. In 1996, "Pistol Pete" was named to the list of 50 Greatest Players in NBA History.

In love with the game even in retirement, he died suddenly while playing in a pickup game on January 5, 1988, at the age of forty. He collapsed from a heart attack and died shortly after that.

WHO ARE SOME OF THE MOST NOTABLE BROTHER ACTS TO APPEAR IN THE NBA FROM THE ERA COVERED IN THIS CHAPTER?

As of a 2019 report on the NBA website, there have been around seventy sets of brothers who have played in the NBA—too many to mention in depth, but here's a sample of some noteworthy brother acts.

Start with the Van Arsdales, the first pair of identical twins to play in the league. They were named (like the Smothers Brothers of comedy fame) Tom and Dick, two graduates of Indiana University. Dick was a three-time All-Star and played for twelve seasons, mostly with the Suns. Tom joined his brother for one year with Phoenix in 1976–1977. At that season's end they both retired from the game. Both averaged more than 15 ppg. while posting almost identical statistics for rebounding average—4.2 rebounds per game (rpg.) for Tom and 4.1 for Dick.

Horace and Harvey Grant are also identical twins, and both were first round draft selections. When Horace was a Bulls teammate of Michael Jordan, he earned three championship rings during the

1990–1992 three-peat wins. He won yet another title with the 2001 Lakers. Horace told *Beckett Basketball* magazine that he would "never get used to playing against someone who looks like me, thinks like me and is a virtual clone of me. We were like cats and dogs about everything, but let anybody else try to mess with either one of us, and we're inseparable."

Another player who won three NBA titles with the Bulls of the Jordan era was John Paxson, brother of Jim, a two-time All-Star who played mainly for the Portland Trail Blazers. Their father, Jim Sr., also played in the NBA back in the 1950s.

There was once a brother act that wasn't a duo or trio, but a quartet of talent in Caldwell, Charles, Major, and Wil Jones. Caldwell enjoyed a long pro (American Basketball Association [ABA] and NBA) career, seventeen seasons. Charles, who won a championship with Houston in 1995, stayed fifteen seasons, while Major spent six seasons in the NBA, two as a teammate of Caldwell with the Rockets. Wil, the oldest brother, lasted a combined nine years in the ABA and NBA.

Gerald Wilkins is the brother of the acrobatic Dominique who was also known as the "Human Highlight Film," a mouthful of a nickname. Dominique was a nine-time All-Star and Hall of Famer who was good for 24.8 ppg. over his fifteen NBA seasons. Toward the end of his career, he played pro ball in Greece and Italy. Gerald was solid, but not spectacular, not unlike a studio backup singer, on the fringe of the spotlight, but he frequently helped his teams produce good records. He lasted thirteen seasons and scored 13.0 ppg. By the way, his son Damien has played in the NBA, as well as leagues in China, Puerto Rico, and Venezuela.

Next are Mychel and Klay Thompson. Mychel only spent one season in the NBA with the 2011–2012 Cleveland Cavs, but Klay has been a mainstay of the Golden State Warriors as a core part of four championship teams. Their father, Mychal, was no slouch, either. The Bahamas native played on two championship Lakers teams of Pat Riley in 1987 and 1988. Mychal is also the father of baseball journeyman Trayce.

Hall of Famer Rick Barry had three sons who played in the NBA: Jon, the oldest of the three, middle son Brent, and Drew. Some of their playing days spilled over into the 2000s, but all began their NBA days before then. Brent turned out to be the best of the offspring, winning the 1996 Slam Dunk Contest, being a part of San Antonio championship squads in 2005 and 2007, and averaging 9.3 ppg.—not bad, but far removed from his father's average of 24.8 ppg. Another brother, Canyon Barry, was in the NBA, sort of. He signed an Exhibit 10 contract with the Minnesota Timberwolves and was waived by them later that day.

Bernard and Albert King are another pair of brothers with one displaying far more skills than the other. Bernard, of course, is a Hall of Famer who carried a 22.5 ppg. average and once led the NBA in scoring at 32.9 ppg. Albert, an Associated Press All-American in 1979–1980 at Maryland, was serviceable, mainly with the New Jersey Nets where he once scored 17.0 ppg.

Other NBA brother combos regardless of era played in include Charles and Dudley Bradley; Ken and Ray Corley; John and Leon Douglas; Bob and Dick Fitzgerald; George and Derrick Gervin; Glen and Grant Gondrezick; Al and Matt Guokas Sr.; Nick and Steve Jones; Eric and Vinnie Johnson; Russ and Ron Lee; Rodney and Scooter McCray; Al and Dick McGuire; Bill and Gary Melchionni; Ed and George Mikan; Calvin and Kenny Natt; Audie and Sylvester Norris; Ed and Charles O'Bannon; Bud and Ralph Ogden; Don and Mac Otten; George and Henry Pearcy; Brent and Mark Price; Jim and Mike Price; Kenny and Phil Rollins; and Campy, Frank, and Walker Russell.

The list rambles on: Steve and Tom Scheffler; Gene and Purvis Short; Chuck and Wesley Person; Brad and Mickey Davis; Connie and Johnny Simmons; Mike and Willie Sojourner; Sam and Tom Stith; Carl and Charles Thomas; George and John Trapp; Jay and Sam Vincent; Michael and Morlon Wiley; Gus and Ray Williams; Jannero and Jeremy Pargo; and *finally*, Marcus and Carl Landry.

WHAT TWO COLLEGE TEAMMATES AND WHAT TEAM MADE NEWS FOR THEIR STUPENDOUS SCORING TALENT?

The 1988–1989 season found Loyola Marymount's Hank Gathers, a 6' 7" forward, earning headlines by leading the nation in scoring at 32.7 ppg. The next year his fellow Lion, 6' 4" senior guard Bo Kimble, upped the ante by scoring at a 35.3 ppg. clip. That average and his 1,131 points led the country and, dating back to 1985, his point total (which shattered the record of Bradley's Hersey Hawkins) has been unmatched.

Incidentally, Gathers's point total from the 1989–1990 season still stands sixth best going back to 1985. However, he outdid Kimble for lifetime points, and his 2,723 markers stands twenty-third for scorers going back to 1948. Plus, he was just the second Division I NCAA player to lead the nation in both scoring and rebounding as a junior.

When these two men played under Coach Paul Westhead, Loyola Marymount was a hoop factory, churning out point after point, scoring 110.2, 112.5, and a mind-reeling 122.4 ppg. That average was 21.2 ppg. ahead of the next most productive team. Of course, Westhead's squad, with its sievelike defense, surrendered an average of 104.2 ppg. over that three-year period. The Lions game was one of run-and-gun, wide-open basketball, for sure. Take 1990, when they once amassed 141 points only to lose to LSU by 7. Furthermore, on December 7, 1989, they engaged in a brawl of a basketball game, accumulating 152 points. Despite that output, they won by a relatively close margin of 15 points over US International.

Obviously, scoring a slew of points isn't everything in basketball. Although Westhead's teams went 74–21 over the Gathers-Kimble era, their highest finish in the AP poll was fifteenth and one year they were unranked at season's end.

Overall, the Lions have been in only five NCAA tournaments, and three of those appearances were in the three years Gathers and Kimble starred. However, those teams lost in the first round, the second round, and in the Regional Final. Still, during their tournament play they really did light up the scoreboard, playing in five of the highest-scoring Men's Basketball Tournament games ever. The highest-scoring game took place in the second round of the 1990 tournament when the Lions and Michigan combined for 264 points, with Loyola running away with a 149 to 115 win over the Wolverines. After holding a slim 7-point lead at the half, Loyola burned the bucket for 84 points over the game's final 20 minutes.

WHAT COLLEGE STAR DIED IN HIS SENIOR SEASON, AND WHAT TRIBUTE DID HIS SURVIVING TEAMMATE GIVE TO HONOR HIS FALLEN FRIEND?

Our look at college stars Gathers and Kimble continues. In his senior season, on March 4, 1990, Gathers collapsed during the West Coast Conference Tournament semifinals versus Portland. He had fallen to the floor earlier that season but seemed to recover fully. This time, he had just put the finishing touches on an alley-oop play when his heart gave out. Two hours later the twenty-three-year-old star was pronounced dead. The cause of death was a heart muscle disorder that restricts the flow of blood.

Kimble and Gathers had played high school ball together in Philadelphia, and they began their college days playing together for the University of Southern California. After one season there, the close friends made it a sort of package deal by bundling up their belongings and moving on to Loyola Marymount.

Grief-stricken at the loss of Gathers, Kimble came up with a way to honor his friend. LMU was playing New Mexico State in the 1990 NCAA Tournament as the declared champs of their conference after the tragedy. Gathers had been a natural right-handed shooter, but after going through shooting woes (lifetime, for example, he shot just 56 percent from the foul line) he switched hands on his shot. Kimble, who normally shot right-handed, decided to do something that would figuratively allow him to be reunited with Gathers. Kimble would shoot the first shot of his tournament games lefty. Although he appeared rather clumsy as he cradled the ball in his left hand before kind of pushing the ball to the hoop, he dramatically sank the unorthodox shot, and the crowd went wild.

Kimble went on to lead everyone in the game in rebounding with 18, and he was the game's high scorer in the 149–115 rout with 45 points, more than doubling the output of the Aggies' top scorer. The Lions made it all the way to the Elite Eight before bowing out to the eventual champs, the University of Nevada, Las Vegas.

Kimble went on the play just three NBA seasons. There are many factors that play into why a college star may be a bust at the next level, including health and injuries, difficulty adapting to the NBA, and a seemingly minor weakness at the college level that catches up to some in the NBA. Kimble averaged 5.5 ppg., scoring just 574 points for his career, about the same number of points he scored in sixteen college games at his peak.

In 2020, just days before the thirtieth anniversary of Gathers's death, the school unveiled a statue of Gathers wearing his retired jersey #44.

WHAT ARE THE HIGHEST-SCORING REGULAR SEASON NBA GAMES—FOR REGULATION PLAY AND FOR OVERTIME GAMES?

On opening day of the 1990–1991 season, the Denver Nuggets lit up the scoreboard at their home arena to the tune of 158 points. Impressive? Well, they lost by four to the Golden State Warriors in the highest-scoring contest ever. The two teams put up 320 points in 48 minutes, an average of 6.67 points per minute, or more than three 2-point field goals per 60 seconds. The Denver defeat was the start of a trend as they finished in last place in the Midwest Division at 20–62. In fact, their pitiful .244 "winning" percentage meant they were the worst team in the entire NBA.

Denver teams back then could always score—they led the league in offense six times in the 1980s. In the 1981–1982 season they became the first team to score 100-plus points in all of their eighty-two regular season games. The catch was they were also generous in giving points away—they led the NBA with the most porous defense five times in that same decade. Early in 1990 they were on the losing end of a 173–143 annihilation at the hands of the Phoenix Suns, who tied the record for the highest score in a non-overtime game. The Suns smashed another record that day when they scored 107 points in the first half alone.

Denver's run-and-shoot coach—not at all surprising—was Paul Westhead, who once commented, "I've always felt I would be the first coach to have a 200-point game ... A team that is willing to run with my team, I don't see why that couldn't happen." Sometimes called "the Guru of Go," Westhead, who won an NBA championship with his 1979–1980 Lakers, never saw his dream come true—his last season as a head coach was 1991–1992.

Golden State's Chris Mullin led all scorers with 38 and Tim Hardaway added 32 while Denver's top scorers were Orlando Woolridge with 37 and Walter Davis with 33. Twelve players hit for double digits, including all five of Denver's starters.

Counting overtime games, the highest NBA output ever was the combined 370 points that ripped the nets as Detroit topped Denver 186–184, in three overtime periods in December 1983. In that game three players hit career highs for points scored: Kiki Vandeweghe with 51, and Isiah Thomas and Alex English both with 47 points.

Pistons coach Chuck Daly joked, "They usually say the first team to 100 will win the game. But in this one, that happened in the middle of the third quarter!"

Meanwhile, the highest-scoring NCAA game ever resulted in nearly *400* combined points when Troy State University overwhelmed DeVry University of Atlanta, 258–141 (for an average of almost 10 points scored per minute), but those are other stories for another book.

HOW LONG DID THE NBA LANGUISH AS FAR AS BEING RECOGNIZED AS REPRESENTING A MAJOR SPORT—EARNING AS MUCH RESPECT AS, SAY, MLB?

That's hard to pin down, but as difficult as it is for modern fans to comprehend, as late as the early 1980s, the league had major problems. In 1982, when there were twenty-three teams in the NBA, seventeen of them lost money. In both 1981 and 1982, the weeknight games of the NBA Finals were not—repeat, *were not*—broadcast during prime time by CBS.

Author Dan Shaughnessy wrote that CBS chose instead to have replays of the games "dumped into late-night slots because they were played during the May sweeps and CBS didn't want to bump their regularly scheduled prime-time programming in favor of a fringe sport." *A fringe sport!*

Even the league itself delayed the beginning of the 1981–1982 season "to avoid clashing with the World Series and to push the start of the Finals past the coveted May sweeps."

WHO ARE ALL OF THE DIVISION I PLAYERS TO LEAD THE NATION IN REBOUNDING AND SCORING IN A SINGLE SEASON?

Only three men have accomplished this feat. The first to do it was Xavier McDaniel, fittingly nicknamed "X-Man." In his senior season (1984–1985) at Wichita State University, he averaged 27.2 ppg. and yanked down 14.8 rpg. Although he made one All-Star team in the NBA, he never reached his college heights again. The twelve-season veteran of NBA play did average 15.6 ppg. as a pro with 6.1 rpg., and he was a member of the 1985–1986 All-Rookie team when he was with the Seattle SuperSonics.

It had taken an eternity for McDaniel to make scoring/rebounding history, but the next man to make this list came along just four seasons later. Hank Gathers of Loyola Marymount matched McDaniel with a hefty average of 32.7 ppg. and 13.7 rpg.—and he did it as a junior. As mentioned, he never got the opportunity to show his skills and see what he could have achieved in the NBA.

The third and so far final man to lead Division I in scoring and rebounding was 6' 9" power forward/center Kurt Thomas of Texas Christian University. During the 1994–1995 season, he came up big with 28.9 ppg. while collecting 14.6 rpg. The man with the odd nickname "Crazy Eyes" spent eighteen seasons in the NBA, mostly with the Knicks, and he scored a modest 8.1 ppg. with 6.6 rpg.

WHO ARE THE PLAYERS WHO LED NCAA DIVISION I PLAY IN BOTH ASSISTS AND SCORING?

First some background. Assists were first recognized as an official stat in the 1950–1951 season. Despite that, from the 1953–1954 season through the 1982–1983 season, no assists leaders were officially noted.

But not long after leaders were singled out, Avery Johnson of Southern University set a record he still holds with his 13.3 apg. average in 1987–1989. His average is excellent as the 10 apg. plateau has been attained just four times (and by only three men). The season before Johnson set the high-water mark, a UNLV player named Mark Wade set another record, still unmatched, for total assists in a season at 406.

Because there were no recognized leaders in this category for so long, Duke University's Dick Groat was denied the official honor of being the first player to lead the country in both scoring and playmaking. But he was an All-American in 1951 and 1952 in both baseball and basketball. He has also been inducted into both the college baseball and basketball halls of fame. He would go on to play baseball in the big leagues for fourteen seasons, with one season in the NBA. In 1952, he was a two-sport man, playing for the Pittsburgh Pirates and the Fort Wayne Pistons.

His jersey number was the first of just a baker's dozen of Blue Devils uniforms to be retired in the rafters of Cameron Indoor Stadium. His #10 was retired in 1952, and the next time a Duke player received such an honor wasn't until 1980. One group named him the college Player of the Year in 1951, and UPI selected him as the 1952 National Player of the Year.

In his junior season of 1950–1951, Groat established a new NCAA record for scoring with 831 points (one source has it as 839 points). The next year, his point total fell a bit to 780, but research indicates that he did lead the country with his average of 26.0 ppg. *and* with his unofficial 7.6 apg. Unofficial or not, the man who once said "I just loved basketball, and I was a much better basketball player than baseball" did what only one other man ever did—lead the NCAA in those two all-important areas.

Two interesting trivia tidbits: Groat once roomed with Richard Nixon's brother at Duke, and one of his Blue Devils basketball coaches, an assistant, was Red Auerbach.

Groat's amazing feats aside, it wasn't until the 2017–2018 season that a player was officially recognized as both the most prolific scorer and passer in Division I play. That man was Trae Young and he did it in his one and only collegiate season. The native of Norman, Oklahoma, stayed local, playing for Oklahoma University right there in his hometown. The All-American and fifth overall pick in the 2018 NBA Draft had a phenomenal freshman season, scoring 27.4 ppg. while handing out 8.7 apg. He shot just over 42 percent from the field and .861 from the foul line.

He hasn't slowed down in NBA play, either. He was on the 2018–2019 All-Rookie team (19.1 ppg. and 8.1 apg.), and in his four years as a pro through 2021–2022 he owns a 25.3 ppg. average and sports an average of 9.1 apg. In the 2021–2022 season he led the NBA in total points scored and total assists, but did not lead the league for most points and assists *per game.*

Young was one of only three freshmen to lead Division I basketball in assists per game played. The other two were T. J. Ford of the University of Texas and Lonzo Ball out of UCLA. And there have only been two sophomores to be the leader in this category: Jason Kidd did it for the University of California and Ja Morant for Murray State.

A year after Young's feat, Morant, a sophomore guard, became the first NCAA player to average 20 or more points along with 10 or more assists.

Final notes: only three men have won the NCAA assists title more than once—Avery Johnson for the 1987 and 1988 seasons,

Jared Jordan of Marist in 2006 and 2007, and Jason Brickman of Long Island University (Brooklyn) in 2013 and 2014. Once, and only once, has there been a tie in the most assists per game stat. That took place in the 2004–2005 season when Portland's Will Funn, a senior, and Demitrius Coleman, Mercer's point guard, averaged 8.0 apg.

WHO ARE THE ONLY TWO PLAYERS TO LEAD THE NBA IN BOTH SCORING AND ASSISTS IN THE SAME SEASON?

For nearly fifty years, Nate "Tiny" Archibald (aka "Nate the Skate") was the only man to shoot often and accurately enough to lead the league in scoring, yet at the same time be savvy and unselfish enough to also lead the way in playmaking. He did this while attempting 26.3 field goals per game, more than double the next "shooting-est" teammate, center Sam Lacey.

In the 1972–1973 season, Archibald piled up 34.0 ppg. to go with his 11.4 apg. He also became, at 6' 1", the shortest player to lead the NBA in scoring. Interestingly, the second-highest scorer that year was the game's tallest player, the 7' 2" Abdul-Jabbar. That season was the first one after Archibald's Cincinnati Royals moved to become the Kansas City–Omaha Kings; they actually played their home games in those two cities.

In the 2021–2022 season, Trae Young made scoring/passing history—*again*—when he joined Archibald in their elite club. Young, just twenty-three years old, proved his college feats were for real as he dished the ball off for 9.7 apg. and fired it through the rim for 28.4 ppg. The Atlanta Hawks sensation has, through his first four seasons, averaged 9.1 apg. and 25.3 ppg.

WHO WERE THE FIRST MEN TO HAVE PLAYED IN AN NCAA TITLE GAME AND LATER COACHED AN NBA TITLE TO A CHAMPIONSHIP?

Both Bill Russell and K. C. Jones were two-time NCAA champs at the University of San Francisco who went on to win NBA titles coaching the Boston Celtics.

Pat Riley also managed this feat, playing for the Kentucky Wildcats when they played in, but lost, the Finals of 1965–1966, then winning NBA crowns with the Los Angeles Lakers (on four occasions) and the Miami Heat. Including his roles as a player, assistant and head coach, and team executive, Riley was a part of nine NBA title winners.

WHO IS THE ONLY MAN TO LEAD TWO MAJOR US PROFESSIONAL BASKETBALL LEAGUES IN SCORING?

That would be Rick Barry. The first time he led a league in scoring came in just his second season in the pros. He upped his scoring average by almost precisely 10 points from his rookie season of 1965–1966 (25.7 ppg.) to a colossal 35.6 the next year. He sat out the next season so he could later jump to the ABA, which he did in 1968, joining the Oakland Oaks. In that first season there, his scoring rampage continued and his 34.0 ppg. led the league.

He must have loved the ABA style of play and, though not to a great extent, its three-pointers, as he is the all-time scorer in that league based upon points per game, 30.5 over four ABA seasons. He still ranks twenty-fifth for all-time scorers with his combined NBA and ABA total of 25,279 points.

Barry was also a member of the last Warriors team to win it all before Golden State became champs again in 2015.

WHO WERE SOME OF THE PLAYERS FROM THE TWENTIETH CENTURY WHO HAD INTERESTING AND/OR UNUSUAL HOBBIES RELATING TO VEHICLES?

Karl Malone was really into monster trucks and big rigs. Once he even owned a trucking company. He could proudly proclaim that shipping cargo with him made sense because, as "the Mailman," he would deliver.

Brad Daugherty's first hobby related not to vehicles but was his love of hunting and fishing. He said he enjoyed almost any outdoor activity and that included water skiing. The seven-footer joked, "I look like a big pole coming across the water." In the year before he entered ninth grade, he underwent a seven-inch growth spurt, from 6' 3" to 6' 10". As for his interest in vehicles, he was attracted to stock car racing, which makes sense given his roots in North Carolina. He even wore jersey #43 to honor racing legend Richard Petty, who had that number emblazoned on his cars.

Daugherty's contract limited his off-season involvement in racing. "I basically just watch. I'd love to do it," he said, adding in a 1993 interview that he planned on racing when he retired. He is part owner of a professional stock car racing team that competes in the NASCAR Cup Series—a team that fields a Chevrolet Camaro ZL1 for Ricky Stenhouse Jr.

A Daugherty teammate with the Cleveland Cavs, Larry Nance was also into cars. In his case, the joy came from the speed of drag racing. "My father was a mechanic," he said. When he broke in with the Phoenix Suns, a friend took him to a race and he said he got bit by the bug. "I think the next week I went out and bought a Camaro." Now his Catch 22 Camaro is adorned with his name, a CAVS logo, and his old jersey number, 22—and drag racing still consumes him.

WHAT TEAM WAS ARGUABLY THE WORST NBA SQUAD EVER?

Based on the worst single-season record of all-time, the Charlotte Bobcats of 2011–2012 are at the bottom of the heap. In the Bobcats' eighth season of existence, many felt this team should have been put out of its misery. Coming off a 34–48 record, what they did the next season made them feel as if they would have died for a 34-win season. They had to settle instead for a pathetic 7-win season. This was a shortened season due to a lockout as a new collective bargaining agreement had to be worked out. The Bobcats' 7–59 record gave them the lowest season winning percentage ever. Or, put it this way, they lost 89.4 percent of their games.

They were so bad that they were mathematically eliminated from any chance to make the playoffs as early as March 28th, with almost exactly an entire month left on their schedule. It had to be a supremely frustrating season for the team's owner as he was a man accustomed to winning over and over again. That man was University of North Carolina alum Michael Jordan. He was also unaccustomed to being treated with scorn, but at the Bobcats' season finale, when his image was shown on the Time Warner Cable Arena's Jumbotron the home crowd lustily booed him.

In another North Carolina tie-in, the Bobcats' two leading scorers, Gerald Henderson and Corey Maggette, had played their college ball in that state, for Duke in Durham, North Carolina.

The former futility record belonged to the 1972–1973 Philadelphia 76ers who won 11 percent of their games, based on their sad record of 9–73. Before that, the worst season-winning percentage belonged to a team from long ago, the 1947–1948 Providence Steamrollers. In their second of just three years in the NBA, they owned a humiliating record of 6–42 for a winning percentage of .125. In their initial season they went 28–32, and *that* was their finest hour. After the six-win season, they improved to winning 20 percent of their games at 12–48 for the third and final year.

WHO WAS THE FIRST BLACK PLAYER IN THE NBA?

This should be a straightforward question, but it's a bit tricky because in a way there are three answers. The very first Black player to be drafted into the NBA—on April 25, 1950—was Chuck Cooper out of Duquesne. In selecting Cooper in the second round of the draft of college players, the Boston Celtics seemingly followed the lead of the Brooklyn Dodgers when they signed Jackie Robinson to a professional contract in 1946. One year later he broke baseball's color barrier in 1947 when he made his big league debut. However, the difference is Cooper wasn't the first Black player to actually *play* in the NBA.

That distinction goes to Earl Lloyd, the Washington Capitols' pick in the ninth round of the 1950 Draft. The small forward out of West Virginia University suited up and played in his first game at Rochester, New York, on Halloween in 1950, one day before Cooper's first contest.

Yet another Black player belongs on the list of pioneers: Nat "Sweetwater" Clifton, the man who signed the first NBA contract. The New York Knicks purchased his contract from the Harlem Globetrotters and got his name on a contract before any other Black player. He made his debut in early November 1950.

The first Black player to be selected to participate in an All-Star game was Don Barksdale for the 1953 showcase contest.

Finally, going back to the old NBL, the Chicago Studebakers was the first team to integrate the game. In the 1942–1943 season (as touched upon earlier, five years before Jackie Robinson joined the Dodgers), they signed six Black players: Tony Peyton, Hillary Brown, Wyatt "Sonny" Boswell, Bernie Price, Roscoe "Duke" Cumberland, and Roosie Hudson.

Prior to these three trailblazers, there were groups of Black teams across the country, commonly known as "the black fives," which insensitively referred to the five starting players on the team. Probably the most notable pro teams like this were the Globetrotters and the New York Renaissance Five, also known as the Rens.

The Rens, according to the *Official NBA Basketball Encyclopedia*, "were spat upon by some fans and insulted by others. Their post-game meals frequently consisted of cold cuts they carried with them in their bus because so many establishments declined to serve them. All this because they were black."

The talented team once put together an eighty-eight-game winning streak, and as they made their way on barnstorming tours, they sometimes played three games in a day. Weary after such days, they were faced with yet another problem—many hotels refused to put them up for a night. So they sometimes had to lug their equipment to the bus for trips of up to 200 miles back to their "command posts in such cities as Chicago and Indianapolis."

Despite all of that, from 1932 to 1936 their record stood at 473–49. In 1939 alone, they won 112 and dropped only 7 decisions. The Rens, formed in 1923, preceded the Globetrotters by five years and stayed together until the team folded in 1949.

WHO WERE SOME OF THE GREATEST LEFT-HANDED PLAYERS OF THE TWENTIETH CENTURY?

Beckett Basketball Monthly listed an All-Lefty squad for players who were active in 1990, then added a star-studded team of all-time greats who were left-handed. The starting five for the 1990 squad consisted of Chris Mullin of the Golden State Warriors and Wayman Tisdale, then with the Sacramento Kings, at the forward spots; San Antonio's David Robinson in the pivot; and guards Johnny Dawkins of the Philadelphia 76ers and John Lucas, who was then in his final season and playing in his third stint for the Houston Rockets.

The bench was made up of three forwards: Sam Perkins, Stacey King, and Michael Cage; along with three centers: James Donaldson, Mark Eaton, and Brad Lohaus; and it was rounded off with just one guard, Sarunas Marciulionis, a man who occasionally played tennis with a racket in both hands.

When it came time to list the greatest left-handed stars from the roots of the game through 1990, they named Hall of Famers Billy "the Kangaroo Kid" Cunningham and Dave Cowens, who actually played center (but did so at just 6' 9"), as the forwards. Since Cowens often employed an effective outside shot, placing him in a forward slot seemed justified.

The starting center was Bill Russell, who won five MVP trophies over one eight-year span. He led the dynastic Celtics to eight straight championships, still the longest such winning binge by any pro team in the United States, and eleven titles over his thirteen seasons in the league.

He also averaged more rebounds for every game than points in each of his seasons, and he had ten seasons in which he averaged 20 or more rpg. Russell also holds the distinction of becoming the first Black head coach in the league's history, taking on that position nearly ten years before Frank Robinson became baseball's first Black manager.

Two southpaw playmakers, also Hall of Fame players, handled the guard chores in Lenny Wilkens, who once was the career leader for assists, and Nate "Tiny" Archibald, who, by the way, was 6' 1" and 150 pounds—truly minuscule by NBA standards.

The all-time lefty list featured a strong bench. Gail Goodrich (18.6 ppg. lifetime), Dick Barnett (15.8 ppg.), and Guy Rodgers (who still ranks high, seventeenth, for career apg. at 7.8) were the guards.

In the meantime, three big men completed the team with Willis Reed, who won the MVP trophy for the regular season, the All-Star game, *and* the playoffs all in the same year (1970); Artis Gilmore, who pumped in 22.3 ppg. over his ABA career, and who led the NBA in field goal percentage four consecutive seasons; and Bob Lanier, who averaged just over 20 ppg. and more than 10 rpg. for his entire NBA career.

Not long after the All-Lefty teams were selected, the 6' 10" Derrick Coleman began to stake his claim as a deserving addition to the list.

WHY IS IT DIFFICULT FOR DEFENDERS TO GUARD LEFT-HANDED SHOOTERS?

Larry Nance, who was a 6' 10" power forward for the Phoenix Suns and Cleveland Cavaliers, explained the difficulties in such matchups. "No matter how many times you go over it in the scouting reports, a left-handed big man has a huge advantage on guys who are used to guarding primarily right-handed guys who usually go to their right when handling the ball. Sometimes in the heat of the game, you don't even know who you're guarding. Or you do, and you just forget that he's left-handed."

John "Hot Rod" Williams, a 6' 11" former teammate of Nance with the Cavaliers, chuckled as he recalled his first encounter with Derrick Coleman. "I had been out injured most of the season and I didn't know much about him. Then I go into the game, and I'm thinking he's going to go to his right like everyone else. Then all of the sudden boom! He goes left and dunks on me. Boy, was I surprised. I ran down the court and turned to Larry [Nance] and said, 'He *is* left-handed. I hope!'"

WHY HAVE SOME OBSERVERS CALLED BILL RUSSELL "THE ULTIMATE WINNER?"

For one thing, Russell, the man with the second-highest total of career rebounds in the NBA, won at least two championships at each of three major levels of basketball play, in high school, college, and the NBA. Plus, he was once the captain of the American team that won in the Olympics.

His high school won two California State titles. Staying on the West Coast, he led the University of San Francisco to two NCAA titles on a team that was so dominant it once strung together fifty-five consecutive wins. There was one more level to conquer before he would enter the world of professional basketball, the Olympics, and his Team USA won the gold in 1956. As mentioned, he went on to win it all in the NBA in eleven of his thirteen seasons there.

His tenacity was never more evident that when it was all on the line. Russell never lost a Game 7 over his NBA career, piling up a 10–0 record in those games. In addition to that, he was 1–0 in a decisive Game 5 of a best-of-five set, meaning that in postseason series that came down to the deciding game, he emerged on the winning team eleven times, never losing once. His record for never losing in games that determined a championship stretches to fifteen when including his two high school and one Olympic titles.

Overall, he played in twenty-nine playoff series and lost just twice, in the 1958 Finals to the St. Louis Hawks of Bob Pettit and Cliff Hagan, and in the 1967 Eastern Division Finals to the eventual champ, the Philadelphia 76ers of Wilt Chamberlain.

Toss in one other feat: as the player/coach of the Celtics for three seasons, Boston won the championship twice.

One surprising negative note: he never finished an NBA season with a field goal percentage of .500 or better. His best mark in that department was a modest .467, and his lifetime percentage was just .440.

BESIDES RUSSELL, WHO ARE THE OTHER THREE MEN TO WIN AN NCAA CHAMPIONSHIP, AND THEN AN NBA TITLE IN CONSECUTIVE SEASONS?

Russell won the NCAA title game with his Dons in 1956, then won his first championship ring with the Celtics to conclude the 1957–1958 campaign. That season he became the first NBA player to average 20-plus rpg. for a season.

The other men on this impressive back-to-back championships list are Henry Bibby, who won a college crown with the 30–0 UCLA Bruins in the 1971–1972 season and won it all again in the NBA as a member of the New York Knicks the next season; Magic Johnson, who took the NCAA title with Michigan State in 1979 in that dramatic win over Larry Bird and Indiana State before going to the Los Angeles Lakers; and Billy Thompson, a key ingredient with the Louisville Cardinals when they won it all in 1985–1986, the season before he was with the NBA champion Lakers.

WHO ARE THE PLAYERS WHO WERE ON COLLEGE AND NBA CHAMPIONSHIP TEAMS (THOUGH NOT IN CONSECUTIVE SEASONS)?

The other men to win it all at the collegiate and NBA levels are listed below in no particular order and with the teams they won their championships with:

Mario Chalmers—Kansas Jayhawks in 2008 and the Miami Heat; Danny Green—UNC in 2009 and the San Antonio Spurs; Arnie Ferrin—Utah Utes in 1944 and the Minneapolis Lakers; Bob Cousy—Holy Cross in 1947 and six NBA titles with Boston; Frank Ramsey—Kentucky Wildcats in 1951 and seven titles with the Celtics; Glen Rice—Michigan in 1989 and the Lakers; Richard Hamilton—UConn in 1999 and Detroit Pistons; Marreese "Mo Buckets" Speights—Florida Gators in 2007 and Golden State; Antoine Walker—Kentucky in 1996 and Miami; Jerry Lucas—Ohio State in 1969 and the New York Knicks; Tom Thacker—back-to-back NCAA titles with the University of Cincinnati and one with the Celtics; Jason Terry—Arizona in 1997 and the Dallas Mavericks; Michael Jordan—UNC in 1982 and six NBA championships with Chicago; James Worthy—UNC in 1982 with Jordan and three titles with the Lakers; Lucius Allen—UCLA in 1967 and 1968 and the Milwaukee Bucks; Gail Goodrich—UCLA in 1964 and 1965 and the Lakers; Keith Erickson—UCLA in 1964 and 1965, and then the Lakers; Jamaal Wilkes—UCLA in 1972 and 1973 and one with Golden State and three more with the Lakers; Lew Alcindor—three straight championships with UCLA from 1967 to 1969, and one title with the Milwaukee Bucks, plus five more with the Lakers (notice the prevalent Los Angeles connection from UCLA to the

Lakers?). Alcindor's win–loss record at UCLA was a jaw-dropping 88–2; Corey Brewer—Florida in 2006 and 2007 and the Mavericks; and Isiah Thomas—Indiana in 1981 and back-to-back championships with the Pistons.

Still others of note—these with additional comments.

Quinn Buckner is one of just seven men to win championships in the NCAA, the NBA, and the Olympics. He was with the Indiana Hoosiers, which remains the last NCAA team to go undefeated when they won it all in 1976. He also came off the Celtics bench when they won the championship for the 1983–1984 season.

K. C. Jones was a player who probably would have been on championship teams in the NCAA and NBA in back-to-back years, but instead of going to the Celtics after being drafted in 1956, he chose to join the US Army. He made that move believing he could not make the 1956–1957 Celtics because they were so deep. Make no mistake, though, he was a fantastic athlete—he once had a tryout with the Los Angeles Rams who saw him as a possible defensive back.

Now, when he did sign on for the 1958–1959 Celtics, he won championships in eight of his nine NBA seasons. He became an NBA Hall of Famer, too. Not bad for a man who scored just 7.4 ppg. and only 3.5 rpg. lifetime—not to mention his lowly career shooting percentages of .387 from the floor and .632 from the line!

Jones, like Russell, won at every level. He won titles in the NCAA, Olympics, and in the NBA as a player, assistant coach, and as a head coach.

John "Hondo" Havlicek came from Lansing, Ohio, a town so small it had no traffic lights, but what it did have was two young men who would become Hall of Famers: Havlicek in basketball and his best friend, Phil Niekro, in baseball as a 300-game winner. Havlicek stayed in state for college and was with the Ohio State team that won it all in 1960, and he won eight NBA titles.

Shane Battier—the 2001 National Player of the Year—helped cut down the net when his Duke Blue Devils won it all that season. He notched two NBA titles with the Miami Heat. He had it all going for him as he also was a three-time collegiate Defensive Player of the Year; he was special off the court, too, as an Academic All American.

UCLA's Bill Walton won the College Player of the Year Award in all three of his seasons with the Bruins, who won the national title with him as their center in 1972 and 1973. He averaged 20.3 ppg. and 15.7 rpg. His win–loss record at UCLA was a marvelous 86–4 (of course it helped to play for John Wooden's juggernaut—his Bruins won ten NCAA championships over twelve years). Walton later won NBA crowns with the Portland Trail Blazers and, in the twilight of his career playing just 19.3 minutes per game, with the Celtics.

Walton will also be forever remembered for his one-man show in the 1973 NCAA tournament in a game versus Memphis State. Despite some foul trouble, he set a new record for the championship game with his 44 points, surpassing Princeton's Bill Bradley, Austin Carr of Notre Dame, and another UCLA Bruin in Gail Goodrich. Remarkably, Walton's points came on 21 field goals on just 22 shots, plus two free throws. His performance was very near to perfection—fans generously overlook his three missed foul shots and easily forgive the one missed shot from the field—and helped give UCLA it ninth national title over ten seasons.

WHAT ARE THE RECORDS FOR THE MOST CONSECUTIVE WINS BY A DIVISION I NCAA MEN'S TEAM AND AN NBA TEAM?

First of all, know this: from 1966 through the 1972–1973 season, UCLA's record was 205–5 (not a misprint)! That means they won 97.6 percent of their games. It also meant they won the national title in all seven of those seasons, giving them claim to the greatest basketball period of dominance ever. As a matter of fact, their *worst*

season during that time period produced a record of 28–2. They went exactly 30–0 in three of those seven seasons.

As for the record for most consecutive games won, that's also an honor owned by the Bruins, and it is a record measured not just by games—a sensational eighty-eight wins in a row—but also by years, as UCLA went from January 1971 until January 1974 without a loss. Their last loss before the streak began was a loss to Notre Dame when Austin Carr scored 46 points, more than half of his Irish's 89 points.

Almost three years later their eighty-eight-game streak ended when number two–ranked Notre Dame trailed by 11 with just 3:22 left to play, yet pulled off a narrow but gratifying 71–70 win over the Bruins. A few of the brightest UCLA stars of the era included Curtis Rowe, Sidney Wicks, Bill Walton, and Jamaal Wilkes.

UCLA also holds the number three spot on the all-time list for consecutive wins with forty-seven from 1966 through 1968. The Bruins were actually coming off what was for them a poor season, with a record of 18–8, and unable to make the NCAA Tournament. They soon returned to form, running off their forty-seven straight wins, but finally fell to the number two–ranked Houston Cougars. The matchup was billed as "the Game of the Century," and it was a battle between the two teams' biggest stars, Houston's Elvin Hayes and UCLA's Lew Alcindor, but Houston squeezed out a 71–69 win in what was then a big deal—a telecast seemingly thrown together at the last minute.

According to NCAA.com, it was "the first regular season college basketball game broadcast nationwide [in 120 markets] in prime time." The attendance at Houston's Astrodome was 52,693, leading to the claim that this was "the largest paid crowd to see a basketball game anywhere in the world . . . ever."

The Bruins eighty-eight-game win streak eclipsed the University of San Francisco's record. The Dons had gone a mediocre 44–48 from 1950 to 1954, so there was little reason to think they were about to set a record, but with Bill Russell, K. C. Jones, and Hal Perry, the team set about chalking up sixty victories in a row from December 17 of 1954 to that exact date in 1956. After winning for such a long time, they dropped four of their five games counting the one that snapped the streak. During their seemingly endless run of wins, they took the national championship in both 1955 and 1956.

Next is the NBA record–winning skein set by the Los Angeles Lakers. That one began on November 5, 1971, and stretched all the way through January 9, 1972. That's a shocking run of thirty-three wins over sixty-five days. They knocked off opponents by an average of 16 points each game. Sadly for Elgin Baylor, the team's streak played out without him, as the aging superstar retired after playing just nine games that season, calling it quits less than a week before the historic run of wins began.

And what a beginning the streak had—a very grueling one. The Lakers won games in three straight nights; they won their first five games in just six days; and after just ten days, they had won eight in a row. As the *Los Angeles Times* points out, "Add in commercial travel the morning following games, and the physical demands were incredible."

The former records for successive victories weren't all that old, with the mark the Lakers broke being just a year old. The Knicks had begun their championship season of 1969 with an eighteen-win tear, and the following season the Milwaukee Bucks broke that record, enjoying a twenty-game stretch of nothing but wins on the way to their NBA title.

After reeling off thirty-three consecutive wins and ending the season at 69–13 (a new record for wins and winning percentage for a season), anything but an NBA title for the Lakers would have been a major disappointment. There was no such letdown. They went home contented, ready for a summer vacation after wrapping up the title in May after going 12–3 in the playoffs against the league's top talents. So, overall, they owned a record of 81–16.

Jerry West said the team was made up of many different personalities, "but when you watch this team on the floor, it was like one mind thinking alike." More on the key Lakers of this season later.

The 2012–2013 Miami Heat squad put up a great effort to tie or top the record but fell six wins shy of a tie despite the talents of LeBron James, Dwyane Wade, and Chris Bosh (they even won ten of their next eleven games to finish the season). Pat Riley coached that team and, interestingly, had been a reserve guard for the record-setting Lakers.

The Warriors came out of the gate to start the 2015–2016 season with twenty-four consecutive wins, lost a game, then rattled off twelve wins over their next thirteen games. They had also mechanically won twenty-eight in a row dating back to the previous year's regular season games. Still, the Lakers record has endured for more than a half a century.

WHAT ARE SOME OF THE IMPRESSIVE WINNING STEAKS SET IN WOMEN'S DIVISION I PLAY?

Begin with the longest winning streak in college basketball exclusively in conference play. That record is held by the University of Connecticut's women's team. They steamrolled opponents for 145 straight regular season games from March 2013 through early February 2022. When their conference tournament games were thrown in, the streak ran to 169 games.

UConn also holds the record for the most consecutive overall wins by a women's team with 111. That—and a résumé that includes twenty-eight conference titles in ACC and Big East play, plus a record eleven NCAA championships, including a three-peat (2002–2004) and a streak of four titles in a row from 2013 through 2016—is mighty impressive.

At the start of the 2022 Women's National Basketball Association (WNBA) season there were sixteen former Huskies on various rosters. The school's overall record through 2021–2022 stands at a lofty 1,240–312 (80 percent winning rate) and they've experienced six undefeated seasons. Since 1995, UConn has produced the AP National Player of the Year on twelve occasions.

WHICH RULE CHANGES CAME ABOUT BECAUSE OF GEORGE MIKAN, WHICH WERE THE RESULT OF WILT CHAMBERLAIN'S IMPACT ON THE GAME, AND WHAT MAJOR NCAA RULE DID KAREEM ABDUL-JABBAR CAUSE?

Many rule changes in the college ranks and the NBA stemmed from the influence of one man, quite often a big man. The 6' 10" Mikan, who wore thick glasses and jersey #99, was so dominant he sent the rule makers scurrying to edit their books. The three-time All-American shot underhand free throws before Rick Barry and Chamberlain and displayed a devastating hook shot long before Abdul-Jabbar came up with his skyhook. He won five championships in just five NBA seasons from 1949 through 1954, and seven pro titles in eight years. He led his league in scoring six seasons running. The marquee at Madison Square Garden once lured fans by promoted the night's event as "Geo Mikan vs. Knicks." He is considered the NBA's first superstar, and no man could stop him.

The rule makers felt they had to find some way to hobble this scoring machine. At least one source claims that Mikan's play led to the origin of the college rule on defensive goaltending in 1944 (as mentioned earlier, an NCAA source differs, saying this rule began in 1945 prompted by the influence of Bob Kurland).

Indisputably, the NBA's first widening of the lane came about due to Mikan. Before 1951, the lane had been 6 feet wide, but in order to shove the massive Mikan farther away from the hoop, it was widened under "The Mikan Rule" to 12 feet. Experts even largely attribute the inception of the 24-second clock to Mikan's presence on courts resulting in opponents' yawn-inducing stall tactics.

It may seem ludicrous, but he was cut from his freshman high school team, thought to be too gauche. His coach chided him, saying, "You just can't play basketball with glasses on. You better turn in your uniform."

When it comes to Chamberlain, begin with one stat to attest to his domineering ways: Michael Jordan hit for 50-plus points in a game thirty-one times in his career, while Chamberlain did this forty-five times—*in one season*. In all, he scored 50 or more points in a positively unbelievable 118 times.

FadeawayWorld.com states that a giant handful of major college and NBA rules were necessitated by Chamberlain's presence. In 1964, the lane was widened again, this time to 16 feet. In college, teammates threw high inbound lob passes from behind their own endline and behind their hoop *over the backboard* for Chamberlain to snag then dunk. That tactic was banned, too. In 1956, offensive goaltending was outlawed (this infraction is now known as basket interference). Lastly, for a time he is said to have "shot" free throws by dunking them! He would take off from behind the line, fly to the hoop, and slam the ball home. A new rule was created stating that "players cannot cross the plane of the free-throw line, even if your feet are not touching the ground, until the ball hits the rim or passes through the basket."

Finally, when Abdul-Jabbar was known as Lew Alcindor, back when he was a high school whiz ready to join the UCLA Bruins, the NCAA decided they had to ban dunk shots for several reasons, with a big one being to hinder the future Hall of Famer. The ban began before the start of the 1967–1968 season and ran for ten years. The NCAA said one reason for the new rule was to curb dunk-related injuries and they griped that the dunk "was not a skilled shot." Alcindor did dunk during his freshman season in college, but not for the varsity team after that. Instead, he would legally hold the ball above the rim, but with his hands outside the cylinder, and drop the ball through the rim, and he soon developed his skyhook as well.

WHO WERE THE GREATEST PLAYERS EVER TO SUIT UP IN ABA ACTION?

In 1997, a special panel which was made up of fifty experts—former sportswriters and radio announcers who covered the ABA, owners, league executives, and fans—selected the All-Time ABA Team.

Not at all surprising, their All-Time MVP was "Dr. J," Julius Erving. Slick Leonard was named the top coach of ABA play.

A select few of the top thirty players include Marvin "Bad News" Barnes, Rick Barry, Zelmo Beaty, Billy Cunningham, George Gervin, Artis Gilmore, Connie Hawkins, Spencer Haywood, Dan Issel, Maurice Lucas, Moses Malone, George McGinnis, Charlie Scott, and David Thompson.

The league was loaded with enough talent to last longer than many groups that try to take on and rival an established league. When the ABA did merge with the NBA, there was certainly a nice influx of talent, and many of the names listed here did some great things in the older, entrenched league.

That meant the established league could no longer mock the ABA with derisive quotes such as, "That [red, white, and blue] ball belongs on the nose of a seal." Nor could the arrogant Red Auerbach make comments such as what he had to say about Dr. J when his ABA play was making everyone gape at him. "Julius Erving, he's a nice player. He might be able to come off the bench in our league." *Nice* player? Seven-time NBA All-Star—*nice*?!

WHO WERE THE BEST THREE-POINT SHOOTERS OF THE ABA?

Things sure have changed over the years. The most accurate ABA shooter from far out was shooting guard Darel Carrier, who could only manage a percentage of .377. He lasted six seasons in the ABA, five with the Kentucky Colonels. He did lead his league twice, but with percentages that nowadays hardly sound impressive, .379 and .375. With stats merged from the NBA and ABA, his career mark of .377 now ranks 163rd.

The next best ABA long shooters were serviceable players Glen Combs, George Lehmann, Louie Dampier, and Billy Shepherd, who are, however, to most fans merely forgotten names from long ago with the exception of Dampier. That 6'-point guard played twelve seasons, including his final three in the NBA. He made seven All-Star teams and helped the 1975 Kentucky Colonels win the ABA championship. He piled up more career assists in regular season play and in playoff games than any ABA player ever. Dampier also scored more points than any other player in the short history of the ABA. All of those feats earned him a spot in the Basketball Hall of Fame.

WITH ALL THIS TALK ABOUT THE ABA, JUST WHEN DID THAT LEAGUE BEGIN, AND HOW WAS IT DIFFERENT FROM THE NBA?

The first game ever held in ABA play took place in October 1967, on a Friday the 13th. It pitted the Oakland Oaks, who won the game, against the Anaheim Amigos.

The other teams in the league's inaugural season were the Pittsburgh Pipers, Indiana Pacers, Minnesota Muskies, New Orleans Buccaneers, Kentucky Colonels, New Jersey Americans, Dallas Chaparrals, Denver Rockets, and the Houston Mavericks.

George Mikan was named the league's commissioner in order to give the ABA an air of respectability and credibility. The league introduced the use of red, white, and blue basketballs and it used the three-point shot (something the old ABL had used). They also employed a 30-second clock as opposed to the NBA's 24-second clock.

The league suffered through typical growing pains, drawing an average of just 2,804 spectators per game at first, and owners' collective losses amounted to around $3 million.

The first season ended, as touched upon earlier, with the Pipers, in their only season in Pittsburgh before moving to Minnesota, as champs. They knocked off the Pacers, the Muskies, and the Buccaneers to win it all.

Some of the ABA's biggest inaugural season stars, in addition to 1967–1968 MVP Hawkins, were assists leader Larry Brown, top rebounder and Rookie of the Year Mel Daniels, and the number one total points producer Doug Moe.

WHAT BROUGHT THE END TO THE ABA?

Some of the stronger teams from the ABA hung on until they could join the NBA, but the year the ABA as an entire league was officially declared dead was 1976. The four teams that were able to cling to life and be adopted by the NBA were the New York Nets, Denver Nuggets, San Antonio Spurs, and the Indiana Pacers.

By the end of the 1975–1976 season, most of the league was in financial shambles, and so many teams had folded there were just seven teams still breathing (some barely gasping): the Spirits of St. Louis, the Kentucky Colonels, the Virginia Squires, and, of course, the Nets, Nuggets, Spurs, and the Pacers.

The league's attrition meant that the playoffs would include five of the seven teams—not exactly an exclusive group. The team with the worst regular season record that was still permitted to play for the title was Indiana with a record of 39–45. The only teams not to make postseason play were St. Louis and the abysmal Squires who managed to win just 18 percent of their eighty-three games.

The ABA lasted from February 1, 1967, through May 13, 1976, when New York won the final championship, and the league included twenty-eight teams in all. So many franchises moved around, and so many folded, that only three of the original teams remained in their same locations for the entire run of the league: Kentucky, Denver, and Indiana. And only three players from the first season were still around when the ABA was (partially) absorbed into the NBA: Byron Beck, Freddie Lewis, and the league's all-time leading scorer, Louie Dampier.

It should be noted that technically the two leagues did not merge—the NBA accepted the four ABA teams and *expanded*. The ABA teams that survived to play in the NBA actually had to buy their way into the league, dismayed at the steep price tag of $3.2 million each.

Remember, too, money was always an issue in the maverick league. Billy Cunningham recalled the days when about 75 percent of the teams struggled to meet their payroll. Players were unsure that they would get their pay, and even with a check in hand, there was doubt. "Guys were running to the bank to be the first to get their checks cashed."

WHAT TEAM IS A PRIME EXAMPLE OF THE LACK OF STABILITY AND CREDIBILITY THE ABA HAD FOR AT LEAST SOME OF ITS YEARS IN EXISTENCE?

Julius Erving began his professional days playing for the Virginia Squires, but in the ABA that meant playing home games in four different venues: Norfolk's Scope Arena, Hampton Coliseum, the Richmond Center, and the Roanoke Arena.

There are quite a few teams that lasted only a short time, but one really good example of an ABA team with no stability and no real roots was the Memphis Tams. That team lasted just two seasons (1972–1974). According to RememberTheABA.com, "the Tams proved over and over again that they were one of the most bizarre teams in professional basketball history."

The existing Memphis team, the Pros, died under the oppressive weight of financial problems. Then along came Charles O. Finley, who already owned baseball's Oakland A's, to keep an ABA team in town.

He vowed to put up a bundle of money and make Memphis "a strong and stable ABA franchise." He then held a contest to select a new nickname for his team and the winner of a $2,500 prize came up with TAMS. The nickname's four letters formed an obscure acronym for Tennessee, Alabama, and Mississippi, supposedly the team's fan base. The logo for the team was an odd one: a floppy hat, or tam-o'-shanter. In the team's debut, Finley had his team and coach prance "onto the floor wearing white, green, and gold tams on their heads."

By December of the Tams' first season, it was discovered that Finley was looking to break his solemn vow. He was negotiating with St. Paul, Minnesota, to carpetbag his team there. The team played home games in places such as St. Paul; Hampton, Virginia; Charlotte, North Carolina; Norfolk, Virginia; Greensboro, North Carolina; Richmond, Virginia; Raleigh, North Carolina; and Cincinnati, Ohio. There was no such place as home, sweet, home for this franchise.

He also began sharp cost cutting. Shortly before Christmas, Finley released veteran Ron Franz, who showed up at the team's offices to pick up his last paycheck. As RememberTheABA.com puts it, "he was told that he would have to turn in his team warmup jacket, duffle bag and suitcase before being paid (Merry Christmas!)." When the season skidded to a halt, Finley promptly had all telephone lines disconnected and closed the offices.

The roster was in as much turmoil as the franchise itself. Over a period of two months in 1972, the team made twenty-four transactions, altering the Tams immensely. When the Philadelphia Phillies once went through a long spell of being the National League's doormat, they had an advertisement on their outfield wall proclaiming, "The Phillies Use Lifebuoy [soap]." Disgruntled fans quipped, "Yeah, and they still stink." Likewise with the Tams, they may have undergone a thorough facelift with all of their trades, but they still reeked, going 24–60, including a 2–15 record to end the season.

Finley delayed hiring a new coach for the following season for so long that the team held just two practices before their exhibition season began. It showed. Their longest winning streak of the season ran for just two games, and over the Tams' two seasons, losing streaks of double digits were not uncommon.

Finley ordered the team to stop handing out game programs, instead giving fans "typed, mimeographed lineup sheets." Attendance plummeted to "lows only previously seen in the ABA with the 1968–1969 Houston Mavericks." The Tams' win total also plunged, down to twenty-one. Eventually, "Finley bailed out and the league took over the franchise." The team, after a name change to the Sounds, lasted just one additional season.

WHO CAN SERVE AS ONE OF MANY EXAMPLES OF HOW A PLAYER TALENTED ENOUGH TO BE NAMED THE NAISMITH COLLEGE PLAYER OF THE YEAR CAN GO ON TO BARELY MAKING A RIPPLE IN THE NBA?

Aside from issues such as health, injuries, and even death (think Hank Gathers and see next item, too), there have been many top-notch college players who could not make the transition to the pro game. Let's take a look at Danny Ferry.

Ferry, a graduate from the famous basketball factory known as DeMatha Catholic High School, gained huge national fame at Duke where he was the College Player of the Year in 1989—just as he had been *Parade Magazine*'s prep Player of the Year four years earlier. In both his junior and senior seasons, he was also the Atlantic Coast Conference (ACC) Player of the Year. As a senior he methodically scored 22.6 ppg. He established school records such as his single game high of 58 points, and he helped take the Blue Devils to three Final Four appearances. He also was the first player in his conference to amass 2,000 or more points, 1,000-plus rebounds, and 500 or more assists. In 2002, he was named to the ACC's 50th Anniversary team as one of the fifty greatest players in the conference's history.

He was the second overall pick in the 1989 NBA Draft by the Los Angeles Clippers, but played a season in Italy for Il Messaggero before joining the Cleveland Cavaliers. He signed a ten-year guaranteed contract with them for $34 million and was, ostensibly, ready to match his winning ways in the NBA.

While he wound up lasting thirteen seasons, and even though he was a fairly decent pro, he was a mere phantom compared to his Duke days. He only averaged in double digits twice with a high of 13.3 ppg., and his career averages for rebounds and points were 2.8 and 7.0 respectively. His average of minutes played per game was almost exactly as long as an NCAA half, 20 minutes.

Warning signs showed early. By his third season, one observer, Nate Thurmond, said, "He's going to have to show his stuff, or else. If you're the number one guy, they'll give you three years to show you're supposed to be a player. They don't *want to*, but they will." He predicted if Ferry didn't improve, "Next year nobody else will want him."

Well, with a ten-year guaranteed contract, Ferry did stay on the job, but, again, with not a great deal to show for it. Thurmond did recognize Ferry's determination and his dedication to the game. "He's the kind of guy who won't give up on himself." And, sure enough, he did plug away for ten more seasons.

Ferry made his presence known beyond his days on the court. Both Danny and his father, an NBA vet, wound up serving as NBA executives. Danny's Cavs teams twice finished with the best record in the NBA, and, with players such as a twenty-two-year-old LeBron James in 2007, Cleveland made it to the NBA Finals for the first time. Under Ferry, the Cavs had a record of 272–138.

WHO WAS THE HIGHEST-DRAFTED COLLEGE PLAYER WHO NEVER PLAYED A SINGLE GAME IN THE NBA? SEE THE PREVIOUS ITEM FOR A CLUE.

Maryland's Len Bias was the second overall pick in the 1986 NBA Draft after averaging 23 points and 7 boards per game. Only Brad Daugherty, a seven-footer out of UNC, went ahead of the 6' 8" Bias. The Celtics, already gifted enough to win the 1986 NBA title, selected Bias with better than pleasant sugar plum dreams of things to come in the very near future.

For Bias, that near future never arrived; his "future" didn't even last as much as two days after the draft. That's when his body was found after he had overdosed on cocaine. He collapsed in a college dorm while he was partying to celebrate his good fortune. He was just twenty-two years old.

WHY DO SOME PLAYERS, MANY BIG MEN IN PARTICULAR, TAKE SO LONG TO DEVELOP IN THE NBA?

Nate Thurmond argues that the old theory, which he addressed in 1992, doesn't hold true. "*Some* big men take longer—some do, some don't. If you're good, you're good. Look at that guy from LSU [then-rookie Shaquille O'Neal]. You can't tell me it'll take him much time." O'Neal scored 23.4 ppg. and snared 13.9 rpg. in his first season to earn Rookie of the Year honors.

He included Kareem Abdul-Jabbar and himself as examples of instant impact players. "I was more fearful of not doing well coming from a [relatively] small school, Bowling Green, than the owners." He was worried during the first few days in camp, and then Wilt Chamberlain joined his San Francisco Warriors group. Thurmond's qualms soon disappeared: "I held my own against him, and I never doubted myself again."

Abdul-Jabbar had been, of course, a standout right from the start, even in high school and college when he went by Lew Alcindor. Not permitted to play varsity ball at UCLA due to the rules of the day, he immediately showed his mettle by leading the freshman team to a decisive 75–60 victory over the Bruins varsity squad in a scrimmage. And remember, that varsity team of 1965–1966 may not have been national champs, but they were good enough to go 18–8, led by Mike Lynn, Edgar Lacey, Kenny Washington, and Mike Warren. Coming off his 31-point, 21-rebound showing versus the varsity squad, Abdul-Jabbar then took UCLA to three straight NCAA titles while being named the tourney's Most Outstanding Player (MOP) all three years.

Warren, by the way, was, at 5' 11", certainly not a big man, but he did go on to play a big (Emmy-nominated) role as an actor on the television show *Hill Street Blues*.

WHAT'S THE ODD STORY BEHIND HOW THE BOSTON CELTICS WOUND UP ACQUIRING FUTURE HALL OF FAME GUARD BOB COUSY?

During the 1950–1951 season, the NBA reduced its number of teams from seventeen to eleven. Players from the six departing teams had to be shipped out to other squads. A dispersal draft was held and it ran well until there were only three players left: two Chicago Stags, high-scoring twenty-five-year-old guard named Max Zaslofsky, and Andy Phillip, a twenty-eight-year-old guard who had been scoring in low double digits, as well as Cousy, a rookie out of Holy Cross who had been drafted by the Tri-Cities Blackhawks.

The *Official NBA Basketball Encyclopedia* states, "There was haggling among New York, Philadelphia, and Boston because no one wanted Cousy. The three names were tossed in a hat and the Knicks got Zaslofsky, the Warriors landed Phillip, and Boston was 'stuck' with Cousy."

Lucky losers. The "Houdini of the Hardwood" went on to help lead the Celtics to six NBA titles and he became a thirteen-time All-Star and a member of the NBA 75th Anniversary Team. He was a supreme playmaker, leading the NBA in assists from his third season through his tenth. He retired as the all-time leader in assists. Coincidentally, when he took over the top spot for career assists, he took over that berth by usurping Andy Phillip.

WHAT TEAM ONCE HAD FOUR GUARDS ON THEIR ROSTER AND ALL FOUR BECAME HALL OF FAMERS?

The Boston Celtics. For five straight seasons, beginning with 1958–1959 until Bob Cousy retired, the Celtics had future Hall of Famers K. C. Jones, Sam Jones, Frank Ramsey, and Cousy in their backcourt—and they won five consecutive NBA championships with those men. Cousy stated such a feat had never occurred before and would possibly never again.

WHO WON THE MVP OF THE FINALS EVEN THOUGH HE WOUND UP ON THE LOSING TEAM?

Jerry West did this in 1969 after putting on a scintillating show for the losing Lakers. He came up big with 37.9 ppg., but he wasn't a "gunner," as he added 7.4 apg. All that wasn't enough to top the Celtics, who won in seven.

He was a shining beacon throughout the playoffs that year, leading everyone in free throws and field goals made, good for 556 points. Furthermore, he unselfishly led all players with his 135 assists.

Winning MVP for a title game or series while playing for a losing team in any sport is a rarity. Only New York Yankee Bobby Richardson achieved this (1960 World Series) in baseball. Likewise, only one NFL player—and not even one who played offense—managed this feat. That man was Dallas Cowboys linebacker Chuck Howley in Super Bowl V.

WHO IS THE MAN WHO SANK THE FIRST SHOT FROM BEHIND THE THREE-POINT LINE IN NBA HISTORY?

The NBA adopted the three-point shot in 1979, and on the first day of the new season, October 12, the Celtics hosted the Houston Rockets in an early contest. Near the end of the first quarter, Boston's Chris Ford canned the first three-point shot in the league's history. Five other players made a shot from beyond the arc that night. Ford went on to hit 42.7 percent of his three-pointers that season. He made seventy of his long-range shots that season to wind up with the third-highest total in the league.

The NBA introduced the new shot on a trial basis for one season before permanently putting the rule in the books. Even at that, the shot didn't take off at first—widespread popularity had to wait. On average, each NBA team made 64 three-pointers on 227 attempts during the 1979–1980 season. The worst long-distance shooting team, the Atlanta Hawks, tried only 75 three-pointers and made a measly 13, for a woeful 17 percent success rate. By way of contrast, in the 2015–2016 season when Stephen Curry set the single season record by firing home 402 treys, he had 886 attempts and he made 45 percent of those tries.

The reliance upon threes has increased markedly over the years. One example: in 1985–1986, Larry Bird led the NBA with 194 attempted three-pointers; in 2018–2019, James Harden set a new record when he threw up 1,028 threes. In the 2021 book *Wish It Lasted Forever*, author Dan Shaughnessy writes, "NBA teams today routinely take more than 40 percent of their shots from beyond the arc." He also noted that in the 2021 All-Star Game, 133 threes "were chucked, almost three per minute."

WHAT ARE SOME OF THE MOST INTERESTING AND/OR COLORFUL NICKNAMES OF NBA PLAYERS FROM LAST CENTURY?

The list is lengthy, even when omitting some obvious ones such as "Magic" Johnson: "Houdini of the Hardwood" for Bob Cousy; Chet "the Jet" Walker; "Cornbread" for Cedric Maxwell; "Dollar Bill" Bradley; "Earl the Pearl" Monroe, "Jumpin' Joe" and "Pogo" for Joe Caldwell; "Truck" for Leonard Robinson; Nat Clifton went by "Sweetwater"; "Clyde" was Walt Frazier; John Havlicek answered to "Hondo"; Wayne Rollins went by "Tree"; and Leonard Robinson was called "Truck"; Jerry West was "Mr. Clutch" and "Zeke From Cabin Creek," while Larry Bird was "the Hick from French Lick."

George Gervin was called "the Iceman"; Charles Barkley was sometimes referred to as "the Round Mound of Rebound," but "Sir Charles" paid more respect to him; there was a "Sleepy" Floyd (really Eric); and a "Downtown" Freddie Brown; Alaa Abdelnaby from Cairo, Egypt, was called "the Pharaoh" and, due to the spelling of his name, "Alphabet"; "Chuck Person was called "the Rifleman"; Darrell Griffith was "Dr. Dunkenstein"; and "the Microwave" was Vinnie Johnson.

Next is a man who went by Kiki Vandeweghe, but his real first name was Ernest, and "Happy" Hairston's given name was Harold; "The Chairman of the Boards" referred to Moses Malone; there was Marvin "Bad News" Barnes and another Marvin in Marvin Webster "the Human Eraser"; David Thompson was "Skywalker"; Shawn Kemp went by "Reign Man"; "the A-Train" was Artis Gilmore; Michael Cage was called "Windexman"; there was Gary "the Glove" Payton; "Popeye" Jones was really named Ronald; and "the Dream" was applied to Dean Meminger and Hakeem Olajuwon.

Derrick "Band-Aid" Chievous's nickname alluded to the fact that he always sported a Band-Aid on the court even though it was there for cosmetic reasons, not medicinal. That practice dated back to his New York City junior high school days when he caught an elbow to his right eye and had a Band-Aid placed over the resulting gash. In his next game, he scored 45 points, and as a *Sports Illustrated* story pointed out, unabashedly including a groan-inducing pun, "He then took to wearing a Band-Aid all the time, and it just stuck with him." Chievous sometimes wore the same adhesive bandage for several days, taking it off at night and, rather like a kid who saves their chewing gum overnight, sticking the Band-Aid to the wall next to his bed.

At first, Pervis Ellison, a star in college at Louisville, earned the cool nickname of "Never Nervous Pervis." Drafted number one overall in 1989, he fizzled due to numerous injuries that sidelined him. That caused a sarcastic change of his nickname to "Out of Service Pervis."

Another man who gained a snide moniker was "Dinner Bell Mel" Turpin. The consensus All-American out of Kentucky was never big on conditioning. On the other hefty hand, he gluttonously answered each and every dinner bell to satisfy his enormous appetite. Basketball-Reference.com lists some of his other food-gorging-related nicknames such as "El Mucho Grande," "Mealman," and "the Great Pumpkin." The site lists him as 6' 11" and 240 pounds, but a news story printed in Turpin's next-to-last season stated he weighed more than 290 pounds around July 1988.

Drafted sixth in the 1984 NBA Draft, not far behind such future greats as Michael Jordan and Charles Barkley, and ten slots ahead of John Stockton, big things were supposed to be looming on Turpin's horizon. Instead, the man who waged a lifelong war with obesity averaged only 19 minutes per game, pulled down a mere 4.6 rpg. and scored a far from hardy 8.5 ppg. Sadly, he died by suicide at the age of forty-nine in 2010.

Like Turpin, another college star who did little in the NBA was a player named Bill Mlkvy (pronounced MILK-vee). Because he came from the Temple Owls, he got the nickname "the Owl without a Vowel."

Going way back to the NBL, there was a player named George Glamack whose eyesight was so poor, he was given the nickname "Blind Bomber."

Finally, there was Lloyd Free, who legally had his name changed to reflect his nickname, becoming World B. Free. He made the change a day before he turned twenty-eight, explaining that his childhood friends in Brooklyn called him "World" when he was in junior high, touting that he was "All-World," and claiming any other label such as All-State didn't do him justice.

Select nicknames from players who spent all or most of their NBA career from 2000 on are in the next chapter.

WHO IS THE ONLY WOMAN TO BE OFFICIALLY DRAFTED BY AN NBA TEAM?

That would be Lusia Harris, drafted by the New Orleans Jazz in the seventh round back in 1977, long before the number of draft rounds shrank. She was also the first person to score in women's basketball history during Olympic play. After being drafted, she was unable to try out for the Jazz because she was pregnant.

She was coming off the campus of Delta State University where she had led her team to three consecutive national titles and a sizzling overall record of 109–6. She was also coming off winning a silver medal during the 1976 Olympics. Yet another honor came her way in 1992 when she became the first Black woman to be inducted into the Basketball Hall of Fame.

Earlier, in 1969, the San Francisco Warriors attempted to draft Denise Long, but the NBA prevented this because, as the league's website states, "she didn't meet the criteria to be drafted—in part because of her gender."

In 1979, there was a woman who actually signed a pro contract. That was UCLA All-American Ann Meyers. Ann was the sister of Dave Meyers who had already starred at UCLA before becoming a Milwaukee Buck (number two pick 1975 NBA Draft). The 5' 9" Ann inked a contract worth $50,000 and the opportunity to try out as a point guard with the Indiana Pacers. *Sports Illustrated* reported that she "held her own, survived the first round of cuts and left an impression that will last forever." The Pacers coach, Slick Leonard, said she was truly better than "a whole bunch" of the male NBA aspirants. The magazine also stated that the Pacers were sincere in picking her, "It was never intended to be a publicity stunt."

The woman who said she "didn't want to be just one of the guys" because her goal was "to be better than them" went on to excel for the New Jersey Gems in the seemingly forgotten Women's Professional Basketball League. One could argue she *was* better than most of the guys because she wound up being inducted into the Naismith Memorial Basketball Hall of Fame.

Trivia item: she married another West Coast star, Hall of Fame pitcher Don Drysdale of the Dodgers organization and winner of 209 games to go with a sparkling 2.95 lifetime ERA.

LONG AGO, WHEN THERE WERE MANY MORE ROUNDS TO THE DRAFT THAN THE CURRENT TWO ROUNDS, SOME TEAMS WOULD MAKE UNORTHODOX, SOMETIMES EVEN ABSURD DRAFT PICKS. WHO ARE SOME PEOPLE CHOSEN WHO FIT THOSE DESCRIPTIONS?

Starting in 1989, the NBA Draft has been reduced to two rounds, the fewest among the four major sports in North America—the NFL Draft and the NHL Draft run for seven rounds and Major League Baseball has twenty rounds. Nowadays, normally only sixty players are taken in the NBA Draft (thirty teams times two rounds).

At one time there were fewer teams in the league, but a decidedly disproportionate number of additional rounds. In reality, teams could continue to select players until each team felt there were no viable prospects remaining. A man could conceivably have been, say, the 239th player selected, which happened in 1970 with Mark Gabriel. That year only fifty-seven of the men drafted made an NBA roster. By way of comparison, in the 2019 and 2020 drafts all but two of the sixty players picked played in the league.

In 1960, the draft dragged on for an almost interminable twenty-one rounds (there were that many true prospects then?). In 1974 the NBA cut the number of rounds to ten. It was reduced to seven rounds in 1985, then to three in 1988, and officially knocked down to two rounds the next year.

With so many picks permitted long ago, some teams had taken the only prospects they felt had a chance to stick pretty early in the draft process. Most teams simply quit making selections at that point. For example, in 1960, from the 14th round on, only the Cincinnati Royals and the Knicks made picks. Then, in rounds 19 through 21, only the Royals continued to choose players.

It's not surprising then that given such freedom to go on and on, there were some picks made for frivolous or sentimental reasons, and some were sheer publicity stunts. It got to the point where, as NBA general manager Al Attles said, "Guys were drafting friends."

When the Royals made their twenty-one picks in the 1960 Draft, they used their nineteenth pick on Larry Willey out of the University of Cincinnati. Given that in his best NCAA season he averaged just 8.1 ppg., 4.8 rpg., and 1.0 apg., plus the fact that he never played a day in the NBA, did the Royals really think he had a chance when they drafted him, or was it a favor to someone, or a sentimental geographic pick?

Not totally related, but an interesting trivia item: NFL Hall of Fame running back Jim Brown was chosen by the Syracuse Nationals of the NBA in the 1957 Draft. He excelled at football, lacrosse, and basketball (15 ppg. as a sophomore) at Syracuse University, so the Nationals were hopeful.

What was labeled a publicity stunt in 1969 by NBA commissioner Walter Kennedy was touched upon in the previous item: the Warriors' thirteenth-round pick of high school basketball star Denise Long. According to StadiumTalk.com, the Warriors *did* draft her, but the pick was voided. She then "played one season in a women's league set up by the Warriors."

In 2013, the Dallas Mavericks owner Mark Cuban told ESPN he would seriously consider drafting All-American Brittney Griner out of Baylor University in the second round of the draft. "If she's the best on the board, I will take her," Cuban told ESPN. When the draft rolled around, the Mavs passed on Griner, leading some to accuse Cuban of grandstanding.

That website also discussed another publicity stunt—the 1977 drafting of Bruce (now Caitlyn) Jenner, Olympic gold medalist in the 1976 decathlon. The Kansas City Kings took Jenner in the seventh round "to mock the Kansas City Chiefs after the NFL team continually said it always drafted the 'best available athlete.'" Jenner had not played basketball since high school, but that didn't stop the whimsical Kings from assigning them jersey number "8616" to correspond to the number of points Jenner racked up in the Olympics.

Bob Beamon was another Olympian drafted by an NBA team. The long-jump world record holder from 1968 until 1991 was selected in the fifteenth round in 1977 by the Phoenix Suns. In 1984, the Bulls chose nine-time Olympic gold medalist Carl Lewis in the tenth round.

When Doug Moe was the Denver Nuggets coach, they drafted four players from Catawba, an obscure North Carolina college where Moe's son just happened to play. Moe, of course, was accused of doing this simply to promote his son's school.

Not long after Larry Brown left his coaching position at UCLA to take over the Nets job, the New Jersey organization drafted Brown's former student manager, Vic Sison, in the tenth round of the 1981 NBA Draft. That kept intact the UCLA streak of having at least one Bruin chosen in every draft dating back to 1964.

Indiana University coach Bobby Knight arranged a tribute for Landon Turner, who had helped the Hoosiers win a national title. About ten months after Turner was paralyzed in an automobile accident, Knight's friend Red Auerbach agreed to draft Turner for the Celtics with the last (225th) pick in the 1982 Draft.

CHAPTER THREE

THE GAME TODAY, IN THE TWENTY-FIRST CENTURY

The game of basketball has grown into gigantic proportions, secure in its place in the minds of millions as the greatest show on earth even though it is played at its most exciting high above the rim and so *above the earth*. The players entertain with more speed, quickness, strength, and savvy than ever before as each generation of the human race gets bigger, faster, and stronger.

This chapter devotes itself to a look at the game today, starting with the 2000 season and focusing on the players, coaches, feats, and events of recent years.

WHAT ARE SOME KEY DIMENSIONS PERTAINING TO THE SPORT OF BASKETBALL IN THE NBA TODAY?

Almost everyone knows that the basketball rim stands 10 feet above the playing surface, but there are more key measurements in the game. For instance, the length of an NBA court is exactly 94 feet, and the width of each court is 50 feet. At midcourt there is the tipoff circle with a radius of 6 feet, which is often adorned with the home team's logo. The lane is currently 16 feet wide, and the free throw line is 19 feet from the endline, but 15 feet from the front of the backboard, which measures 6 feet wide by 42 inches in height.

PerformanceHoops.com states that the three-point line does not form a perfect arc. "Instead, the three-point line runs in a straight line from the baseline out 16 feet, nine inches, at which point the line begins to curve. The straight lines are an even 22 feet from the center of the basket, and on the arc, the distance is 23 feet and nine inches." The smallest dimension on courts is the width of the actual free throw line at two inches.

Kids sometimes wonder if two basketballs can fit into a rim at the same time, and the answer is no, not in men's play. The standard diameter of a basketball used by men's leagues including high school, college, and the NBA is about nine and a half inches and rims are eighteen inches in diameter. However, BasketballWorld.com confirms that two women's basketballs can "fit through a basketball rim at the same time within a quarter of an inch to spare."

WHO ARE SOME OF THE BEST BROTHER ACTS TO APPEAR IN NBA ACTION FROM 2000 ON?

First, a quick fact. According to DunkOrThree.com, the odds of anybody making it to the NBA are about the same as the Celtics of the Bill Russell era losing to the Sisters of Charity Five—so slim that only about one hundred out of sixteen thousand college players will end up in the league. By extension, the chances of a family producing two or more brothers to play at the highest level are about the same as the Washington Generals rattling off a long win streak.

The Antetokounmpo family was blessed with a ton of talent. Four brothers—if you count Alex, who actually never appeared in an NBA game but was signed to a contract by the Toronto Raptors in October 2021, only to be waived just two days later—all born in Athens, Greece, were in the NBA. Plus, another brother, Francis, played professional soccer.

Start with Giannis, "the Greek Freak," born in 1994. The winner of two MVP awards, he led his Milwaukee Bucks to the championship in 2021, just one year after earning the Defensive Player of the Year Award. Even though he had played fewer than ten seasons, he was impressive enough to make the NBA's 75th Anniversary Team.

Thanasis is two years older than Giannis, and he also won his NBA championship in 2021 playing alongside Giannis. Finally, there's Kostas, who was born in 1997. With an NBA title as a member of the Lakers to his credit in 2020, the brothers were part of two consecutive championship teams.

Identical twins Markieff and Marcus Morris even have identical tattoos. They reportedly also share a bank account. In 2011, Markieff was the thirteenth overall pick in the NBA Draft, and his brother was chosen five minutes after him at number fourteen. The two former Kansas Jayhawks were even teammates with the Phoenix Suns for around two-and-a-half seasons.

Caleb and Cody Martin also are twins who both played their prep ball for Oak Hill Academy, then suited up for North Carolina State before moving on to play for the University of Nevada. Brook and Robin Lopez, born on April Fool's Day in 1988, make up another set of identical twins. They also have the distinction of being twins who each stand 7' tall. Brook was a teammate of Giannis and Thanasis Antetokounmpo on the championship Bucks team.

How's this for a topper: on December 28, 2019, the New Orleans Pelicans met the Indiana Pacers, and that game featured not two, but three brothers. Jrue Holiday was with the Pelicans while Justin and Aaron suited up for the Pacers.

Pau Gasol, a 7' center/power forward, and his brother Marc Gasol, a 6' 11" center, combined for nine All-Star berths and three NBA titles. The Barcelona natives won other honors including a Rookie of the Year Award for Pau in 2001–2002, and the Defensive Player of the Year Award for Marc in 2012–2013. Oddly enough, the two were once traded for each other.

Duke gave the NBA two brothers in Tre and Tyus Jones. Tyus was the Blue Devils point guard in 2014–2015, and Tre held that same position for two seasons, beginning in 2020. Blake Griffin, now with Boston, had a brother, Taylor, who also spent a season in the league with the Phoenix Suns.

Of course, the Curry brothers, Stephen and Seth, stand out. Their sister, Sydel, married Damion Lee, making him their brother-in-law. Lee had been a Warrior teammate of Stephen's for four seasons starting in 2018. Finally for the Curry family, Seth married Doc Rivers's daughter, Callie, so he has another famous brother-in-law, NBA guard Austin Rivers.

Then there are LaMelo and Lonzo Ball, along with Jalen and Jaden McDaniels, cousins of Juwan Howard. Next are Ben and Tyler Hansbrough; Zoran and George Glamack; Mason, Marshall, and Miles Plumlee; Stephen and Joey Graham; Jeff and Marquis Teague; Brandon and Kareem Rush; and identical twins Jason and Jarron Collins.

The trio of Luke, Tyler, and Cody Zeller; as well as Derek Fisher and Duane Washington (plus Duane Washington Jr.); Juancho and Willy Hernangomez; and J. R. and Chris Smith round out this list of NBA siblings.

WHAT MAN ASSEMBLED THE LONGEST STREAK OF SCORING MORE THAN 20 POINTS IN EACH GAME?

Wilt Chamberlain went 126 consecutive games with 20 or more points. The streak ran from October 19, 1961, to January 19, 1963, when he was with the Warriors. As if that wasn't enough, he also strung together 92 games with 20-plus ppg. stretching from February 1963 to March of the following year.

Other players with long streaks include Oscar Robertson with 79 and Michael Jordan and Kevin Durant with 72. Durant led the NBA in scoring four times, which ties him with Allen Iverson and George Gervin for the third-most scoring titles.

At the start of the 2022–2023 season, Paolo Banchero, the number one overall draft pick of the Jazz, scored more than 20 points in each of his first six games to tie fellow Duke alum Grant Hill, along with Dominique Wilkins and Oscar Robertson for third place on the list of rookies to make such an immediate splash in the NBA. Elvin Hayes scored 20 or more points in his first ten NBA contests, but the record holder once more is Chamberlain, who did this over each of his first fifty-six games. Banchero, at age nineteen, is the youngest of the above-mentioned stars.

WHO HOLDS THE RECORD FOR RACKING UP THE MOST SEASONS IN WHICH HE AVERAGED AT LEAST 20 PPG.?

LeBron James. His twenty such seasons through 2021–2022 outdistances the next two men on the list by three. He stands ahead of Moses Malone and Kareem Abdul-Jabbar. The next most prolific men on the list tied with fifteen seasons are Kobe Bryant, Kevin Durant, and Michael Jordan.

James broke into the NBA in 2003 and averaged 20.9 ppg. as a nineteen-year-old. Though he surprisingly only once led the league in scoring, he has never had a season in which he scored beneath his rookie average. Three times he has reached the 30 or more level.

AMONG MEN WHO WERE ACTIVE DURING THE 2021–2022 SEASON, WHO ARE THE PLAYERS WHO BELONG TO THE 20,000-POINT CLUB?

In the 2022–2023 season, LeBron James shot by Kareem Abdul-Jabbar's all-time record of 38,387 points. James's average point total per game played (27.21) is the fifth-best ever, trailing Michael Jordan at 30.12; Wilt Chamberlain, 30.07; Elgin Baylor, 27.36; Abdul-Jabbar, 27.28; and just a tad above Kevin Durant at 27.18 through 2021–2022.

Predictably, James is also the most productive scorer among active players in postseason play with 7,631 points. That means if you count playoff points with regular season points, nobody has ever scored more points than James with over 46,000. He eclipsed Abdul-Jabbar in 2021–2022 in this category, and ranks well above the third-, fourth-, and fifth-best scorers: Karl Malone, Kobe Bryant, and Michael Jordan.

To be fair to the old-timers, long ago there weren't as many playoff rounds and therefore not as many games as are now played. One example: James has played in 266 playoff games over his first nineteen NBA seasons, and Jerry West played in 153 postseason contests during his fourteen seasons of play.

Final notes on James: he does trail one man, West, when it comes to the most points ever scored during NBA Finals. West scored 1,679 in such games—that's a 30.5 ppg. average over nine Finals. Sadly, for that superb player, his Lakers went 1–9 in the Finals, losing eight times before taking the title in 1972. Through the playoffs held in 2022, James won four of the ten Finals in which he appeared and averaged 28.4 ppg. He also became the first player in the NBA to lead both teams playing in the Finals for scoring and assists. That took place in 2015 when his Cavs met the Warriors.

Other active players (through 2021–2022) who have topped the 20,000-point plateau are Carmelo Anthony, fairly close to the 30,000-point level with 28,289; Durant (25,526); James Harden (23,477); Russell Westbrook (23,298); Chris Paul (20,936); LaMarcus Aldridge (20,558); Joe Johnson (20,407); and Stephen Curry with 20,064. Closing in with more than 19,000 points are DeMar DeRozan and Dwight Howard. In all, there are fifty-three men with 20,000 or more points in NBA/ABA action.

WHO IS THE NBA'S GREATEST PURE SHOOTER OF ALL TIME?

Few experts would argue strongly, if at all, against Stephen Curry. That's especially the case if the definition of being the best shooter entails canning myriad long bombs (as well as sinking free throws with robotic precision). And this man makes the nets sing out a melodic *swish* from anywhere on the court.

On December 14, 2021, the Golden State sharpshooter broke Ray Allen's record for three-pointers made. Curry didn't just break the mark, he absolutely breezed by Allen, especially considering Curry needed just 789 games to compile his 2,974 treys, while Allen required *511 more games* than Curry to reach his record.

Upon smashing the mark, the man with the feathery touch commented that looking forward it would simply be a case of "how far can you push it." The way he was going, and then at the age of thirty-three, he had a whole lot of shoving left to do. He is, of course, the only player ever to top the 3,000 three-point field goals made.

Even while playing on a talented team, Curry has, as one writer puts it, at times been capable of "winning games all by himself." Through the 2020–2021 season, and not counting the 2019–2020 season when he was limited to just five contests, he has only once had a three-point field goal percentage under 42. He has finished in the top ten in that department eight times.

His pure shooting form also places him first all-time for free throw percentage at 91 percent. That places him above such other great deadly shooters as Steve Nash, Mark Price, Peja Stojakovic, Reggie Miller, and Larry Bird, for example.

By coincidence, Curry and another all-time luminary, LeBron James, were both born in Akron, Ohio, though three years apart.

ACCORDING TO ONE SOURCE, WHAT TWO MARKSMEN MAKE UP THE "BEST-SHOOTING BACKCOURT IN NBA HISTORY?"

It's arguable, of course, but in the book *Basketball: A Love Story*, the best shooting guard duo is "the Splash Brothers," Curry and Klay Thompson. The book calls Curry "a slight, baby-faced sniper," and loves his one-two punch with the 6' 6" Thompson.

Their most productive season came in 2015–2016 when Curry led the league with his 30.1 ppg. and Thompson chimed in with 22.1. Not many guard duos can give its team 52.3 points each night. That season, Golden State averaged 114.9 points per game, best in the NBA, meaning the two starting guards provided coach Steve Kerr (and his interim coach Luke Walton for forty-three games that year) with 45.5 percent of their total points.

ONCE MORE, BASING MATTERS ON BEST PERCENTAGE SHOOTING, WHO ARE THE TOP PLAYERS EVER WHEN IT COMES TO, IN EFFECT, NOT MISSING THEIR SHOTS?

The people with the highest two-point field goal percentages are not, like the three-point artists, deadeye shooters as their success at making so many of their shots is usually based upon their nearness to the hoop. In other words, to state the obvious, the most accurate shooters are the people who make their living in the paint.

Seven of the top ten players on the list were centers, and two of them were listed as being a center/forward. Only the number ten man, Amir Johnson, doesn't fully fit the profile—and even he is listed as a small forward/center/power forward.

Another pattern emerges in this area as four of the five men on this list were active in 2021–2022 and all five of them were active as late as 2019–2020.

Number one on the list is DeAndre Jordan (.674), who broke in with—and spent most of his time with—the Los Angeles Clippers. He is followed by Rudy Gobert of the Utah Jazz (.655), journeyman Montrezl Harrell at .630, Clint Capela of Houston and more recently Atlanta with a .625 two-point FG percent, and Tyson Chandler, a veteran of eight teams, at .598.

WHO ARE SOME SELECT PLAYERS WHO SPENT MOST OR ALL OF THEIR CAREERS FROM THE YEAR 2000 ON WHO HAVE COLORFUL, INTERESTING NICKNAMES?

James Harden is "the Beard"; Luka Doncic is "Cool Hand" Luka; "Time Lord" refers to Robert Williams; Yao Ming was called "the Great Wall"; "Mad Dog" is Mark Madsen; Davis Bertans is "the Latvian Laser"; Chris Andersen went by "Birdman"; Robert "Tractor" Taylor got his leviathan nickname because he was 6' 8" but made scales groan with his 284-plus pound bulk; Trajan Langdon was "the Alaskan Assassin"; Paul Pierce is "the Truth"; Dwyane Wade can go by "D-Wade" or "Flash"; Matt Bonner was mainly called "Red Rocket" and "Red Mamba"; "Mr. Big Shot" is Chauncey Billups; "the Claw" refers to Kawhi Leonard; "KG" or "the Big Ticket" are labels for Kevin Garnett; Kristaps Porzingis goes by several nicknames, including "Unicorn" and "Zinger"; the same is true of Jason Williams, aka "White Chocolate" and "J-Dub"; "Linsanity" is Jeremy Lin; Vince Carter was called "Vinsanity" along with other names such as "Air Canada"; Joel Przybilla goes by "Vanilla Gorilla" and "Ghostface"; "the Matrix" alludes to Shawn Marion; one of Tim Duncan's nicknames is "Groundhog Day"; while one of Kobe Bryant's nicknames was "Black Mamba"; Kevin "KD" Durant also goes by "Slim Ripper" among about five other names; Allen Iverson was "the Answer"; of course, everyone knows "King James" refers to LeBron James, aka "the Chosen One."

WHAT ARE SOME OF THE LONGEST NCAA TOURNAMENT GAMES OF ALL TIME?

In 1956, Canisius played North Carolina State in the first round of the tournament. By going into quadruple overtime, that contest remains the longest March Madness affair ever. Hank Nowak scored 29 points for the winning Golden Griffins of Canisius in the 79–78 victory. The game was marked by an unfruitful third overtime session which wound up scoreless, leaving frustrated Wolfpack fans to wail, "Oh, if we had only made one measly bucket from the field or even from the line."

Six years later, St. Joseph's and Utah tied the marathon record in the game played to determine the third-place team in the tournament. These consolation games were discontinued in 1981. St. Joseph's, led by Jack Egan's 42 points, put 15 points up in the fourth overtime to 8 for Utah, winning a slugfest, 127–120.

Five March Madness contests lasted for three overtimes, and UNC took part in two of them. Arguably, the most famous of the five exhausting games occurred the last time UNC played Kansas prior to 2022. That was their 1957 thriller—that is to say, the *second* thriller that year. The odds of playing back-to-back triple overtime games are astronomical, but that's exactly what happened with North Carolina.

The Tar Heels had topped Michigan State in the national semifinal game, winning by scoring 8 points to 4 for the Spartans in the third overtime stanza. They then advanced to take on Kansas and their dazzling centerpiece player, Wilt Chamberlain, who would later be named the tournament's MOP.

WHO WON THE 1957 NORTH CAROLINA VERSUS KANSAS TRIPLE OVERTIME CLASSIC, THE LONGEST GAME IN NCAA CHAMPIONSHIP HISTORY?

Many observers felt Kansas would certainly win what author Joe Gergen called "the most fascinating, most compelling and most bizarre championship game in the annals of the NCAA Tournament." After all, they had the player who was the most dominating player around in Chamberlain. He was intimidating in every aspect of the game, averaging 29.6 ppg. in his first season of 1956–1957, and 30.1 in his next, and final, year with Kansas. He owned the boards, too, averaging 18.9 and 17.5 rpg. in college play. Surely, he would lead the Jayhawks to the championship.

However, there were also many experts who looked at UNC and saw the team had held on to the number one ranking in the polls since January 21, the first poll in which Kansas, coached by Dick Harp, dropped from their top status to number two.

One point to remember about the matchup is that Carolina coach Frank McGuire used some basic psychology on Chamberlain and his own players, too. Before the game began, McGuire basically told his team that Chamberlain was just too much to handle. "I said he was so good, maybe we better not show up. I said he might stuff some of them through the basket with the ball. I said we didn't have a chance unless our entire team defensed him at all times, and he'd still probably beat us so bad it would be embarrassing to go home." He later explained, "Of course, I was kidding them, and they knew it, but it was psyching them up and loosening them up at the same time."

As for psyching out the proud Chamberlain, McGuire chose Tommy Kearns to jump center versus "the Big Dipper." Kearns stood 5' 11"—more than a foot shorter than Chamberlain. Gergen wrote that the move was "a comic masterstroke that ridiculed the Jayhawks' major asset and brought smiles to his own players."

By fronting Chamberlain and having his forwards attempting to seal Chamberlain from the basket, McGuire's defense prevented the big man from scoring until the clock read 4:48 in the opening half. As would occur in 2022, UNC was hot in the first half, shooting 64.7 from the field, while Kansas struggled, hitting just 27.3 percent of their shots from the field.

UNC led by seven at the intermission, but the game was knotted at 46 at the end of regulation play. Both teams scored just two points in the first overtime period and none in the next period. The Tar Heels pulled it out, 54–53, to run the table, finishing the year with an untarnished 32–0 record to 24–3 for the Jayhawks. UNC was just the second undefeated NCAA team to win the championship, and the first ever out of the ACC.

Lennie Rosenbluth, who was named to the All-Tournament Team, led all UNC scorers in both triple overtime games with 31 then 20 points (even though he fouled out late in the second half of the championship game) to wind up at 26.9 ppg.

In the meantime, the words of Coach Harp's predecessor, Phog Allen, haunted Jayhawk fans. Allen had predicted, "We could win the championship with Wilt, two sorority girls and two Phi Beta Kappa's." Maybe so, but not *this* championship, not against *this* UNC squad.

The Tar Heels endured, winning triple overtime games on consecutive nights—this was before the final two games were held on a Saturday and the following Monday. Yes, Chamberlain had a game high of 23 points and, with 14 rebounds, had accounted for half of his team's boards. But, as Coach McGuire, who would later coach Chamberlain in the NBA, put it, "We had the better team. We played him, not Kansas. We beat Kansas, not him."

Trivia note: the 2021–2022 Tar Heels defeated Duke to move on to the title game against Kansas. The two bitter rivals who are about eight miles apart in the state of North Carolina had played each other 257 times over a period stretching back almost a hundred years to 2020. Incredibly, they had never met in the NCAA Tournament. Of course, there are factors involved here such as the fact that for years only one team from a given conference was permitted to play in the tournament. That rule stayed on the books until several months after the 1973–1974 season concluded. Two teams per conference were then permitted to join the tournament's annual dance.

Still, it seems hard to fathom that it took so long for them to meet in March Madness competition. They came close in 1991, with both teams making it to the Final Four but in opposite brackets. A dream duel was foiled when Kansas dismissed UNC. Duke's final path to that season's title featured their defeat of UNLV, then winning it all with a 72–65 win over Kansas.

Final note: Chamberlain's field goal percentage as a collegiate (.470) was surprisingly low. In the NBA he shot .540 for his career and led the league in that category nine times, including his final two seasons, and in six of his last eight seasons. He was successful on just over 68 percent of his shots in 1966–1967 when he guided his 76ers to the championship, and he even topped the NBA at the age of thirty-six at .727 in his final season.

In the 1967–1968 season, perhaps thinking, "I have nothing left to accomplish or prove concerning my ability to score at will and rebound like nobody else; but to prove my all-around talent, I'm going to concentrate on my passing game," he led the NBA in assists with 702 (8.6 per contest). He remains the only center ever to accomplish that.

WHEN THE NCAA ADDED FAN FEST ACTIVITIES TO MARCH MADNESS, THEY JUICED UP THE ALREADY ELECTRIC FINAL FOUR WEEKEND. WHAT ACTIVITIES THAT APPEAL TO BOTH KIDS AND ADULTS GO ON DURING FAN FEST?

In 2022, fans were given the opportunity to see legends up close in the New Orleans Ernest N. Morial Convention Center. Former Duke All-American Christian Laettner put on a Buick-sponsored clinic, pulling young fans out of their bleacher seats and onto a basketball court to go through some drills. Among other highlights of his clinic was having kids help him reenact the famous Grant Hill-to-Laettner pass that led to Laettner's stunning game-winning shot to defeat Kentucky in the 1992 Elite Eight pairing.

Hill also made an appearance at a Nissan-sponsored event during the 2022 Final Four Fan Fest, and he absolutely delighted his followers. When he popped into a tent to greet fans, an organizer, wanting to shield Hill from excessive attention, had told the crowd that Hill would meet them briefly and shake hands, but they had to move on quickly and no pictures were to be taken.

Hill graciously overrode the decree, saying he would be glad to give autographs and pose for pictures. "I'll sign," he said. Then the thoughtful Hill added, "I brought my own Sharpie." He then spent ample time with everyone, patiently signing, posing, and listening to the predictable stories they felt they just had to share with him: "I was there when you threw that long pass to Laettner to beat Kentucky," or "I'll never forget that alley-oop dunk off Bobby Hurley's pass in the 1991 title game against Kansas."

There were also cheer clinics, interactive games, autograph and photo opportunities, including fans being able to snap a selfie with the NCAA championship trophy, and even a Home Run Derby. There were plenty of giveaways, from sunglasses, Reese's Pieces shirts, scrub hues, and Final Four drawstring backpacks, to free Wilson basketballs for youngsters.

Fan Fest is always an impressive showcase for the game. During previous special events surrounding the 2000 Final Four weekend, Harlem Globetrotter Michael "Wild Thing" Wilson established a world record when he dunked on a hoop that stood 12 feet high.

HOW RARE IS IT FOR TWO TEAMMATES TO EACH PUT UP THIRTY OR MORE FIELD GOAL ATTEMPTS IN AN NBA PLAYOFF GAME?

In May 2022, two Milwaukee Bucks turned this trick when Giannis Antetokounmpo and Jrue Holiday each fired off a whopping thirty shots in Game 3 of their Eastern Conference Semifinal series against the Boston Celtics.

This marked the first time this occurred since June 13, 1993, when both Michael Jordan and Scottie Pippen each accounted for thirty-plus shots for the Chicago Bulls. That game wound up being a win for the Phoenix Suns in triple overtime. The last time two teammates each attempted thirty or more field goals in a regulation playoff contest took place way back in 1965.

In the Bucks–Celtics game in 2022, Antetokounmpo, Milwaukee's first round pick in the 2013 NBA Draft, went off for 42 points (16-for-30) in a 102–101 win. Holiday supported him with 25 points on 11-for-30 shooting.

BASED ON 2021–2022 SALARIES, WHO ARE THE HIGHEST-PAID PLAYERS IN THE NBA, AND HOW DO THEIR EARNINGS COMPARE TO OTHER PLAYERS?

Rounding off salaries a bit, Stephen Curry's contract called for him to get paid $45.8 million for the 2021–2022 season. James Harden and John Wall were tied for the next spot at $44.3 million. Next came Russell Westbrook, getting by on $44.2 million that season. The fifth-highest-paid NBA star was Kevin Durant at just a bit over $42 million.

Rounding out the top ten were LeBron James ($41.2 million), Giannis Antetokounmpo ($39.3 million), and three men who earned just $70 less than Antetokounmpo—Damian Lillard, Kawhi Leonard, and Paul George.

By way of contrast, during the 2000–2001 season the top three earners were Kevin Garnett at $19.6 million, Shaquille O'Neal at $19.3 million, and Alonzo Mourning at $16.9 million.

The lowest NBA salary for the 2021–2022 season was $925,258, with players who signed a ten-day contract getting a paycheck of $53,176. The minimum salary paid to a player who had ten or more years of experience was way above the $925,258 amount, but, by Curry standards, a minuscule $2,641,691. That amount is also far off what the average NBA player grossed, right around $8.5 million.

HOW LONG DOES THE AVERAGE NBA GAME, WHICH RUNS 48 MINUTES ON SCOREBOARDS, ACTUALLY TAKE TO PLAY?

Over the last five years or so, the average game length is approximately 2 hours and 13 minutes. It should be noted that average does not include overtime contests. Also, some rules implemented for the 2021–2022 season in an effort to speed up games seemed to have had no real effect (at least not based on the small sampling of one year). Regulation games played the year before the changes were made ran one minute shorter than those played in 2021–2022.

A study indicated that the tighter the game, the longer it takes to play. That only makes sense as close games usually result in more intentional fouling down the stretch as well as more strategic time-outs being called by both coaches. Blowouts usually run 10 or more minutes shorter than games in which the winning team winds up with a victory margin of 1 to 5 points. Televised regular season games don't run as long as playoff games due to the myriad commercial breaks TV executives pack in for postseason contests.

WHAT WAS SO REMARKABLE ABOUT THE WARRIORS WINNING THE NBA TITLE IN 2022?

A lot of things. For one, Golden State went to the Finals five straight seasons from the 2014–2015 season through the 2018–2019 campaign. Then they hit the skids the next season, finishing with a record of 15–50 and a .231 winning percentage, the worst in the entire league. The following season they did improve, but only up to a fourth-place division finish with a 39–33 record. To go from their nadir to winning another championship just two seasons later is amazing.

Furthermore, they pulled off the clinching win in Game 6 in dramatic style. They reeled off a string of 21 unanswered points against the Celtics for the longest such streak in the Finals over the last fifty years.

Additionally, the nucleus of the team, Stephen Curry, Klay Thompson, Andre Iguodala, and Draymond Green, took home their fourth championship ring in 2022—perhaps not as unbelievable as the Celtics of the Bill Russell era, but truly an outstanding accomplishment. The dynamic foursome had won titles in 2015 and 2017 with sixty-seven regular season wins (.817 winning percentage), and in 2018. They became the first team to win four titles over an eight-year period since Michael Jordan's Chicago Bulls won six from their 1991 championship through their 1998 title. The only other teams to record similar dominion were Russell's Celtics in both the 1950s and 1960s, and the Lakers of Magic Johnson, which won the 1980 title and then four more through their championship of 1988.

In 2022, the Warriors won 65 percent of their regular season games to finish second in their conference to mark the only time they didn't win the Western Conference over the recent seasons featuring title runs.

WHAT RATHER SHOCKING THING HAPPENED TO STEPH CURRY (AND HIS INCREDULOUS FANS) IN GAME 5 OF THE 2022 FINALS?

Going into that contest, Curry owned several record streaks, and they all ended that day. Curry was unable to sink even one shot from beyond the arc. That marked his first game without a trey since November 8, 2018, a period of just over forty-three months. He was coming off a 43-point outing in Game 4, but went 0-for-9 from the three-point range in his next game.

It was quite noteworthy as it was the first time he ever came up empty on threes in an NBA postseason game. He had run his streak of making at least one long-range shot to 233 regular season and post-season contests before it was halted. Previously, he set a record with 196 consecutive games with at least one trey, and his current record of 233 in a row is more than double the best streak by any other player. Plus, he owns the record for having sunk at least one three-pointer in 132 postseason games, a streak dating back to 2013. His record of 38 straight playoff games with more than one three-pointer also ended.

He shook off the death of his streaks, glad that his Warriors had drawn to within one win of another championship. "I don't think I've ever been happier after a 0-for-whatever type of night." In the next game, the sixth and deciding contest, Curry shot 6-for-11 from long distance and took high scorer honors with 34, tied with Boston's Jaylen Brown.

Trivia sidenote: had the Celtics defeated the Warriors in the Finals, they would have won their eighteenth championship as a franchise, which would have snapped a tie they have with the Los Angeles Lakers.

HOW MANY TEAMS THAT HAVE WON AN NBA CHAMPIONSHIP DID SO BY SWEEPING THROUGH THE PLAYOFFS WITHOUT A SINGLE LOSS?

No team has ever managed this. The closest a team came to a playoff sweep came in 2016–2017 when the Warriors won four in a row against Portland, Utah, San Antonio, then three more versus Cleveland to go 15–0. Needing one more win for the clean sweep, Golden State finally dropped a 137–116 decision in Cleveland's Quicken Loans Arena. Going into that loss, the Warriors had won every postseason game by a convincing average of 16 or more points, and only three of their opponents had lost by less than 10 points. They did win the title with a brilliant 16–1 postseason record.

The champion Lakers of 2001 were 11–0 in the playoffs as they went into the Finals versus Philadelphia. They lost Game 1 by six in overtime, then went on to take four games in a row. In 1983, the 76ers won it all by going 12–1 in playoff action, losing only in Game 4 of the Eastern Conference Finals against the Milwaukee Bucks.

History lesson: the first year it required a team to win fifteen games in order to claim the championship was 1983–1984. From the 1965–1966 season up to the 1984 title, it took twelve wins to become champs. Before then, there were years when the title winners only needed a handful of victories. For example, the first NBA champions, the 1946–1947 Philadelphia Warriors, played three rounds and needed just eight wins to take home the title.

It's never easy to win the championship, but few people realize that when the Celtics won their first eight titles, they needed to play in just two rounds of the postseason. So when they won their first championship in 1957, they played just ten games, going 7–3.

Nowadays, if a team was forced to go seven games in each of their rounds on the way to winning it all, they would have played twenty-eight contests.

WHEN THE NBA ANNOUNCED ITS 75TH ANNIVERSARY TEAM IN 2021, HOW MANY OF THE GREATS OF THE GAME PLAYED AT LEAST ONE FULL SEASON IN THE TWENTY-FIRST CENTURY? HOW MANY WERE STILL ACTIVE DURING THE 2021–2022 SEASON?

Eleven men were active in 2021–2022: Giannis Antetokounmpo, Carmelo Anthony, Stephen Curry, Anthony Davis, Kevin Durant, James Harden, LeBron James, Kawhi Leonard, Damian Lillard, Chris Paul, and Russell Westbrook.

The other stars who played into 2000 and beyond are Ray Allen, Karl Malone, Kobe Bryant, Patrick Ewing, Michael Jordan, Shaquille O'Neal, David Robinson, Dwyane Wade, John Stockton, Scottie Pippen, Steve Nash, Gary Payton, Hakeem Olajuwon, Paul Pierce, Dirk Nowitzki, Reggie Miller, Tim Duncan, Jason Kidd, Allen Iverson, and Kevin Garnett.

The players represented on the 75th Anniversary Team owned a cumulative 158 NBA championships, 730 All-Star selections, 110 MVP Awards and Finals MVPs, and they accounted for more than

1.5 million points. Every member of the 50th Anniversary Team from 1996 made it for the 75th Anniversary Team as well.

Only four men have been named to all four anniversary teams, the 25th (when only ten players were selected), 35th, 50th, and the 75th. They are Bill Russell, Bob Cousy, George Mikan, and Bob Pettit.

The super 75th Anniversary Team also had players from six countries and territories including Antetokounmpo (Greece), Duncan (U.S. Virgin Islands), Ewing (Jamaica), Nash (Canada), Nowitzki (Germany), and Olajuwon (Nigeria).

The league set up the following selection rules: The team "was selected by a blue-ribbon panel of current and former NBA players, coaches, general managers and team and league executives, WNBA legends and sportswriters and broadcasters. Voters were asked to select the 75 Greatest Players in NBA History without regard to position. Panelists did not rank their selections. Current and former players were not allowed to vote for themselves."

WHO WAS THE LOWEST DRAFT PICK TO WIND UP WINNING AN MVP AWARD?

When Nikola Jokic of the Denver Nuggets won the MVP in 2020–2021, he became the lowest draft winner so honored. He promptly won the award the following season as well. Denver didn't get around to selecting him until the forty-first choice in the second round of the 2014 NBA Draft.

The Serbia-born Jokic, a 6' 11" center, exploded for 26.4 and 27.1 ppg. in his MVP winning seasons. He also led his league in rebounding in 2021–2022 after finishing fifth in the league the year before that. He once even finished third in the NBA for assists.

WHO HOLDS THE WNBA RECORD FOR WINNING THE MOST THREE-POINT CONTESTS?

That mark belongs to Allie Quigley of the Chicago Sky. In the 2022 competition held in Chicago, she sizzled the net from far out, giving the thirty-six-year-old Quigley back-to-back championships in the three-point event. In the final round she put up 30 points, nine more than the next best score of Ariel Atkins of the Washington Mystics. Quigley thus earned her fourth three-point title, one more than NBA record holders in this department—Larry Bird and Craig Hodges. Jay Cohen of the Associated Press wrote that her fourth win stamped her "as one of the greatest shooters in the history of the league."

Over her career, she has shot close to 40 percent from beyond the arc, almost exactly 50 percent on her two-point field goal attempts, and just a bit shy of 90 percent from the foul line.

CHAPTER FOUR

MISCELLANEOUS WHO, WHAT, WHEN, WHERE, WHY, AND HOW

Some topics don't fit neatly into the time frames of the preceding chapters. Here, then, are "leftover" or miscellaneous items.

WHO ARE THE PLAYERS WHO HAVE HAD THEIR JERSEY NUMBER(S) RETIRED BY MORE THAN ONE NBA TEAM?

The list of men who had their jersey numbers retired by two different teams are Nate Thurmond (42, Warriors/Cavs); Oscar Robertson (1 and 14, Bucks/Kings); Julius Erving (6 and 32, 76ers/Nets); Kareem Abdul-Jabbar (33, Bucks/Lakers); Clyde Drexler (22, Trail Blazers/Rockets); Elvin Hayes (11 and 44, Wizards/Rockets); Michael Jordan (23, Bulls/Heat—see explanation below); Bob Lanier (16, Pistons/Bucks); Earl Monroe (15 and 10, Knicks/Wizards); Dikembe Mutombo (55, Nuggets/Hawks); Shaquille O'Neal (34 and 32, Lakers/Heat); and Jerry Sloan (4 and 1223, Bulls/Jazz—see explanation on next page).

Two men were honored by three teams—Wilt Chamberlain's 13 was retired by the Warriors, 76ers, and Lakers; and Pete Maravich's 44 was put in mothballs by the Hawks, and his 7 was retired by the New Orleans Jazz and Pelicans.

Only Maravich and Michael Jordan have had their numbers retired by a team they never even suited up for. The Pelicans paid tribute to Maravich as a thanks for what he contributed to the game of basketball in Louisiana. As for Jordan, the Miami Heat retired 23 for the same basic reason as Maravich, for contributions made to the game, and the Bulls retired that number for more obvious reasons. Like Major League Baseball did to show their appreciation to Jackie Robinson when his 42 was retired by every team, the NBA did the same with Bill Russell's 6.

WHAT ARE SOME OTHER INTERESTING FACTS ABOUT NBA PLAYERS (AND OTHERS) WHO HAVE HAD THEIR JERSEY NUMBERS RETIRED (OR GIVEN A SIMILAR SIGN OF GRATITUDE)?

Let's begin with an oddity: Nate Thurmond, who spent only about 12 percent of his career in Cleveland (but like LeBron James is from nearby Akron), was honored by having his number retired as an individual and, along with fellow members of the 1975–1976 Cavs, he was honored again by the team. "I think I made an impact. The first time they painted our numbers on the floor," said Thurmond. "The next time uniforms were raised to the rafters. I pushed back a tear, even 15 years later. It was chilling."

Other men have experienced the same thrill Thurmond spoke of—even some others who never wore their teams' uniforms—and that even includes owner Walter Brown, founder of the Celtics, who was unofficially given a #1 banner. The Hawks raised a banner to recognize team owner Ted Turner (and retired a number for Atlanta mayor Kasim Reed). Pistons owner William Davidson got the same type of celebratory respect as did Larry Miller, owner of the Utah Jazz.

Many coaches and executives are on this list of honorees: Boston's Red Auerbach, Utah's Frank Layden, Phil Jackson of the Bulls, and Red Holzman of the Knicks—his number is 613 for the total wins he registered for New York. Likewise, Doug Moe's number is 432 for his wins guiding the Nuggets, and Bobby Leonard had his 529 retired to commemorate his wins with the Pacers. Jerry Sloan's win total of 1,223 with the Jazz earned him the highest number of them all. Trivia aside: the lowest retired jersey number belongs to Celtics center Robert Parish, who donned the unusual 00.

Flip Saunders has a "FLIP" banner for his work as the Timberwolves head coach. Chuck Daly of the Pistons was assigned #2 for his two NBA titles. Portland's head coach Jack Ramsay was given #77 to symbolize the 1977 NBA title he won for the Blazers. The Bulls also recognized general manager Jerry Krause, just as the Pistons did with GM Jack McCloskey. Carroll Dawson's work as an assistant coach and general manager earned him a banner with the initials CD. The Suns recognized coaches Cotton Fitzsimmons and John MacLeod, and they even singled out team athletic trainer Joe Proski.

Another group of nonplayers who gained honors includes the arena public address man for the 76ers, Dave Zinkoff, and broadcasters Johnny Most of the Celtics, Joe Tait with the Cavs, Don Poier of the Memphis Grizzlies, Chick Hearn with the Lakers, and Bill Schonely for Portland. Johnny Most, as one example, had no number, of course, but a cloth microphone is stitched into a Boston Garden banner to pay tribute to him.

Marques Johnson was a four-time All-Star for Milwaukee, but perhaps part of the reason the team retired his #8 was to also pay respect for his work as a television color analyst since 2015. Another former Buck, Jon McGlocklin, called "The Original Buck" by some, also wore Milwaukee's jersey (#14) and also sat behind a mic to broadcast games (1985–2018).

A few other broadcasters to join the list are Al McCoy of the Suns, Bob Blackburn of the SuperSonics, and Hot Rod Hundley for his work with the Jazz.

In 1988, a rather large group of people were recognized when the Sacramento Kings retired #6 as a sign of appreciation for their unofficial sixth man, their fans. The Magic did the same thing for their fans even though the team did allow Patrick Ewing to take that number when he joined the team for his last year in the NBA and his only season with Orlando (2001–2002). That season his usual jersey number, 33, was being worn by teammate Grant Hill, who had already been with the team.

Another oddity took place when a player's jersey was retired after he had unretired. It played out like this—Sidney Moncrief called it quits before the 1989–1990 season. Midway through that season the Bucks retired his uniform. Three days before the start of the following season the Hawks lured him back into duty, which meant he was the only active player with a retired jersey on his résumé.

Boston's Jim Loscutoff did not have his #18 retired (Dave Cowens would later, though). Instead, the Celtics retired his nickname "Loscy" by hoisting a banner over the Garden floor. He got that recognition even though he averaged just 6.2 ppg. and 5.6 rpg. over his nine seasons.

The Heat did a curious thing when they retired Dan Marino's #13 for the impact he made on the city as a member of the Miami Dolphins. They did not, however, really *retire* that number as it has been worn since 2017 by Heat star Bam Adebayo. By the same token, Trail Blazers owner Larry Weinberg was assigned an honorary #1 jersey, but that number is still made available to players (Anfernee Simons has worn that number of late).

The Knicks retired #15 to honor both Earl Monroe and Dick McGuire. The Trail Blazers paid tribute to two men who wore #30, Bob Gross and Terry Porter. Then there was one team, the Lakers, who created an NBA first when they retired two jersey numbers for the same man, Kobe Bryant, for his numbers 8 and 24.

As would be expected, the Celtics have retired the most numbers at twenty-five. Only three teams have yet to retire a player's number, the Los Angeles Clippers, and two teams with a comparatively short history, the Toronto Raptors and the Memphis Grizzlies.

WHO WAS THE MOST DURABLE AND PERHAPS THE MOST AGELESS NBA PLAYER EVER?

Wilt Chamberlain was an iron man, never needing rest—and in the 1961–1962 season that would have been a 100 percent literal statement: he never once left a game due to fatigue or, for that matter, foul trouble.

That 1961–1962 season vividly showcased his stamina as he averaged 48.5 minutes played per game, which leads to a math problem. Take the number of minutes in an NBA game, 48, and ask: is Chamberlain's 48.5 greater than or less than 48? How can someone play more minutes than a regulation game contains?

The answer is actually pretty easy. His Philadelphia Warriors played in five overtime contests, with one going into double overtime and another lasting three overtime sessions. Chamberlain played for the entire game in seventy-nine of his team's eighty regular season games, missing time only when he was ejected from one contest during the third quarter.

This is not to say he possessed Superman's invulnerability. At the age of thirty-three, an injury limited him to playing in just twelve games, and over one span of two seasons he only played in seventy-three games. However, for his career he averaged 45.8 minutes played per game, and he led the league in minutes played nine times, even managing this when he was thirty-two years old.

Further evidence of his ageless quality came long after his retirement. Onetime UCLA coach Larry Brown tells the tale of the days when Magic Johnson brought Laker teammates James Worthy, Norm Nixon, Byron Scott, as well as Bernard King to the Bruins campus for pickup games in the early 1980s. Chamberlain, well into his forties, would have four college players for teammates to oppose Johnson's all-stars.

With a game tied and with one bucket to go for the win, Johnson put up a running hook shot that Chamberlain rejected. Johnson declared it was goaltending. Game over. Chamberlain disputed Johnson's declaration and asked Brown to make the call. Brown said he didn't believe there had been goaltending on the play.

At that point, Brown said Johnson "starts screaming and yelling, takes his ball, yells, 'Next!' Wilt grabs the ball from him and says, 'We're gonna play another game, and there'll be no more shots taken at this basket.' And he proceeded to block [every subsequent shot]."

The most ageless person in league history as far as being active at a very advanced NBA age is Nat Hickey. He qualifies because he played in the BAA at the age of forty-five, but this distinction is tainted. In 1948, he was coaching the Providence Steamrollers and, with his team's record at 4–25, he decided to add himself to the active roster. He played in two defeats, shot 0-for-6 from the field, and scored on just two foul shots.

The man who truly deserves recognition for ageless play is Kevin Willis, who was forty-four when he finally retired, ending a career that extended from 1984 through a small portion of 2007 (aside from his one year "retirement" in 2005–2006).

Vince Carter deserves a tip of the hat for his longevity. He was still active at the age of forty-three, but more significant, he played in parts of four decades, an NBA first. Fewer than a dozen players have hung around long enough to log twenty or more seasons, and Carter is at the head of the list with twenty-two seasons played (1999–2020). He broke the record of twenty-one seasons that had been shared by Willis, Kevin Garnett, and Dirk Nowitzki.

Carter sat out the night when he first became a four-decade man three days into the new year of 2020. His Hawks coach, Lloyd Pierce, commented, "He's old. I think it's crazy in the sense that he's played longer than some of our guys [have been alive]."

Atlanta teammate Trae Young told the *Athletic*, "He may not be the high-flyer he used to be, but he's smarter than 80 percent of the players that are on the court when he goes out and plays, regardless of who is on the court. That's what happens when you put in so many years and the older you get."

BASED SOLELY UPON SHOOTING PERCENTAGES, WHO ARE THE GREATEST THREE-POINT SHOOTERS OF ALL TIME?

Well, it's *not* Stephen Curry, who, in fact, trails his own brother in this realm. The man who sank the highest percentage of treys ever was Stephen Curry's head coach on the Golden State Warriors, Steve Kerr. The multitalented Kerr came as close as anyone to making half of his three-point attempts at .454.

Mathematically, if a player made 50 percent of a hundred shots from two-point range, he contributed 100 points to his team's efforts. A player taking one hundred three-point shots has to make thirty-four shots to be worth more to his team, for 102 points, than the man taking shorter, supposedly *easier* shots. For every one hundred treys Kerr launched, he hoisted 135 points onto the scoreboard for his teams—and he played for six teams. This was one player whose steamer trunk was cluttered with his many destination decals.

The peripatetic Kerr broke in with the Phoenix Suns in 1988–1989, a year later he was traded to the Cleveland Cavs for Kevin Johnson. He played briefly for the Orlando Magic before settling in with the Chicago Bulls. He later played for the San Antonio Spurs and the Portland Trail Blazers. Incidentally, Kerr's lifetime two-point field goal percentage stands at .494, exactly 4 percent better than his deep shooting percentage.

Trailing Kerr as the best lifetime three-point shooters are Hubert Davis (.441), Seth Curry (.440), Joe Harris (.439), and Drazen Petrovic (.437). Some fans may be surprised to learn that Larry Bird shot *only* .376 to rank 172nd on the all-time list. Likewise, the former record holder for the most career three-pointers, Ray Allen, ranks only 46th on the lifetime list based on his .400 percentage.

WHAT TEAM OWNS THE RECORD FOR THE MOST WINS DURING A REGULAR NBA SEASON?

Not counting their fifteen postseason wins, the 2015–2016 Golden State Warriors won seventy-three of their eighty-two games for a stunning winning percentage of .890 to break the record set by the Chicago Bulls of the 1995–1996 season (.878) when they went 72–10 and then rolled on to 15–3 in the postseason.

Don't forget that the Bulls had tremendous success the following year, too, when they won sixty-nine games. The NBA champion Bulls from both of those seasons were led, of course, by Michael Jordan, who had great support, mainly from Scottie Pippen and Dennis Rodman. The Bulls' sixty-nine wins in 1996–1997 remains tied for the third-most wins with the 1971–1972 champion Los Angeles Lakers, which starred Wilt Chamberlain, Jerry West, Gail Goodrich, Happy Hairston, and Jim McMillian. Chamberlain was also on the team, the 76ers, which had previously set the single season win record of sixty-eight in 1966–1967, when they won the NBA championship.

Returning to the Bulls and Warriors success stories, the Bulls' seventy-two-win season record looked untouchable at first, and it did remain as the single season high for twenty years. Then along came the Warriors of 2015–2016. The nucleus of that team was made up of Stephen Curry, Klay Thompson, and Draymond Green.

They not only won seventy-three games that year, but that season was sandwiched between two seasons in which they won exactly sixty-seven contests *and* won the NBA championship both years.

The season during which they set the current record they fell in the Finals to the Cleveland Cavaliers of LeBron James, Kyrie Irving, and Kevin Love. Only the Warriors and the 1972–1973 Celtics have ever won sixty-eight or more games in the season yet were eliminated in the playoffs.

WHAT TEAMS SHARE THE RECORD FOR THE MOST HOME WINS IN A SINGLE SEASON?

Both the San Antonio Spurs of 2015–2016 and the Boston Celtics of 1985–1986 won a marvelous total of forty home games versus only one defeat. The Spurs of head coach Gregg Popovich were led by Kawhi Leonard, LaMarcus Aldridge, Tony Parker, and a thirty-nine-year-old Tim Duncan. They wound up winning twenty-seven road games to go 67–15 overall. However, they lost in the Western Conference Semifinals to the Oklahoma City Thunder, which featured Kevin Durant and Russell Westbrook.

Meanwhile, the Celtics featured the superlative crew of Larry Bird, Kevin McHale, Robert Parish, Dennis Johnson, and company. Like the Spurs, this crew won sixty-seven times during the regular season then went on to topple Houston and their Twin Towers of seven footers Hakeem Olajuwon and Ralph Sampson for the NBA title.

WHAT TEAM OWNS THE BEST ROAD RECORD FOR A SEASON?

The Warriors of 2015–2016 went 34–7 in away contests. They excelled at home as well, going 39–2, and, as mentioned, they advanced to the Finals where they lost to the Cavs in seven games. They won the first two games of the series, both at home in the Oracle Arena, built up a three-wins-to-one lead, but lost Game 5 at home. Uncharacteristically, they lost another home game in the series-deciding contest. Golden State led by one point going into the last quarter but wound up losing, 93–89.

Recently, the Phoenix Suns made a run at the Warriors' record, but fell short, going 32–9. They had that same record in home games and were led by high scorers Devin Booker and Deandre Ayton.

WHAT NBA TEAMS MADE THE PLAYOFFS, BUT DID SO WITH THE LOWEST WINNING PERCENTAGE EVER?

The worst team to still be given a chance (albeit a very slim chance) to win the NBA crown was the 1952–1953 Baltimore Bullets. They won just sixteen games of their seventy contests played for a so-called winning percentage of .229! Their defense was ranked tenth in the ten-team league, and their offense wasn't much better, seventh. They played the Knicks in the opening round of the postseason and were dispatched in two straight games.

Seven season later, the Minneapolis Lakers managed to win just one-third of their games (25–50). In the playoffs, they swept the Pistons in the Western Division Semifinals (best of three), then took St. Louis to a seventh game before bowing out. Not even the presence of all-time great Elgin Baylor, who averaged just under 30 ppg. (29.6), could take these Lakers very high.

The third-worst playoff team was the Chicago Bulls from the 1967–1968 season. They wound up with a 29–53 record (.354) even though the team had seven players average in double figures, led by Bob Boozer's 21.5 ppg.

WHO SCORED THE MOST POINTS IN A SINGLE PLAYOFF GAME?

Twelve times a player has scored 55 or more points in a playoff contest, and on half of those occasions the player hit for exactly 55 markers. Those who topped that level are Charles Barkley, Wilt Chamberlain, and Michael Jordan tied at 56; in 2007, Donovan Mitchell added his name to the exclusive list with 57 points; Elgin Baylor pumped in 61 points in a 1962 game and that record stood until the current record holder, Chicago's Jordan, poured in 63 in a 1986 game versus the Celtics. That was a double overtime 135–131 loss in which Jordan played 55 minutes. He hit on 22-of-41 from the field and 19-of-21 from the line.

It should be noted that the record for the most points in a Finals game is still the 61 points Baylor put up in Game 5 in 1962. That year he also set the record for the most total points in a Finals series, 284 in seven games.

WHO HAS SCORED THE MOST LIFETIME POINTS IN POSTSEASON PLAY?

LeBron James has, through the 2021–2022 season; he accumulated 7,631 points, way ahead of Jordan's 5,987 and Kareem Abdul-Jabbar's 5,762. Of course, players from long ago—take Jerry West and his 4,457 playoff points—had far fewer opportunities to appear in the postseason than today's players. As mentioned earlier, James engineered his points over fifty different series and 266 games (28.7 ppg.). By way of contrast, Jordan played in thirty-seven series and 179 playoff games (33.4 ppg. which is the highest postseason average ever), and West made it to only twenty-eight series and 153 total contests (29.1 ppg.).

WHO ARE THE ONLY ROOKIES TO LEAD THE NBA IN SCORING?

In the 1959–1960 season, Wilt Chamberlain, then with the Philadelphia Warriors, averaged 37.6 ppg., gaudily announcing that a Goliath of a man had entered the league. That average remains the highest ever for a rookie. He scored almost exactly 6.5 points each game above the second-leading scorer, Cincinnati Royals small forward/shooting guard Jack Twyman.

Elvin Hayes left the University of Houston campus, joined the San Diego Rockets roster as the overall number one selection in the 1968 NBA Draft, and breezed to the scoring title with a 28.4 ppg. average as a not-so-raw rookie. He is also one of just eight rookies to score 50 or more points in a game. Despite his spangled stats, Hayes did not cop the Rookie of the Year Award (see next item).

The very next season along came a man who, in college play, gave Hayes several memorable battles. That man was Lew Alcindor. He didn't exactly match Hayes and Chamberlain, but the man who would soon change his name to Kareem-Abdul Jabbar did become a rare first-year NBA player to lead all scorers—*for total points*—but not for the highest scoring average. In that 1969–1970 season, Abdul-Jabbar scored 2,361 points to average 28.8 ppg., but future Lakers teammate Jerry West was the official scoring leader with his 31.2 ppg.

Likewise, in Michael Jordan's rookie season of 1984–1985, he scored more points than any other NBA player (2,313), but his average of 28.2 ppg. fell short of leading scorer New York small forward Bernard King. King, who averaged 32.9 ppg., played in just fifty-five games to Jordan's eighty-two but qualified as the scoring champ, which was based on a minimum of seventy games played or 1,400 points.

WHO WERE THE ONLY PLAYERS TO WIN THE MVP AWARD AS ROOKIES?

Only Chamberlain and Wes Unseld of the Baltimore Bullets have ever won the MVP Award as rookies. Chamberlain's Warriors were a fourth-place team at 32–40 without him in 1958–1959. With the fantastic rookie, they went 49–26 to capture second place in their division.

Unseld took home the MVP trophy for his toil in the 1968–1969 season. His Bullets had finished in fourth place with a 36–46 record the year before his arrival in town. With him, they shot up to a 57–25 record and won the NBA Eastern Division title.

Due to his lack of height, Unseld was an interesting center. He was a solid 245 pounds, but stood only 6' 7". When he played against, say, Abdul-Jabbar, he gave away seven inches, but the future Hall of Famer out of Louisville had skills. He was adept at setting picks with his wide body (some called him "The Oak Tree"), unleashing great outlet passes, forcefully grabbing rebounds (his 14.0 rpg. lifetime still ranks sixth in NBA play), and, in short, helping his teams win.

As was expected, both Chamberlain and Unseld also won the Rookie of the Year Award. Overall, sixteen men who won the Rookie of the Year Award went on to, at some point, win an MVP Award, but what Chamberlain and Unseld did was quite special.

WHAT ARE PLAYERS' ATTITUDES CONCERNING SIGNING AUTOGRAPHS FOR FANS? AND WHAT ARE PLAYERS' REACTIONS WHEN THEY ARE ASKED TO SIGN ONE OF THEIR BASKETBALL CARDS AND THEY GAZE AT THEIR IMAGE ON THE CARD?

The range of their attitudes is quite wide. Some players simply don't want to be bothered signing anything for anybody, while others do so grudgingly, knowing it is part of the expectations placed upon them. Former Cleveland Cavs five-time All-Star Brad Daugherty represents the other end of the spectrum.

"I sign all the autographs I can. I sign all of them through the mail and after a game if I get an opportunity. It's flattering. I mean, if someone wants your autograph for the recognition of your work, then that's wonderful."

Even when he was coming off a bad day, he said, "It doesn't take but a couple of seconds to sign an autograph, you may make someone's day, and it's worth it if you can do that."

As for players' reactions to their cards, again, some sign the cards with nary a glance at the image, but Daugherty said, "It's really funny to see myself on a card and all this [information] about me on a card. And I see little kids with them, wanting me to sign. I guess it's really a sign that you've arrived. That's what you think once you see yourself on a basketball card. It's a lot of fun."

WHAT IS SO UNUSUAL ABOUT THE BASKETBALL PROGRAM AT ST. FRANCIS UNIVERSITY, A SCHOOL WITH AN ENROLLMENT OF ONLY ABOUT 2,400 OR SO STUDENTS?

Hardly a famous basketball factory, this rural university has nevertheless sent five players to the NBA. What makes this unusual is that while only three became stars, two of those men wound up leading the league in assists—coincidence or good recruiting by St. Francis?

The two great playmakers were Norm Van Lier and Kevin Porter. Van Lier joined the NBA in 1969 with the Cincinnati Royals and took top assists honors the next season. He passed for 10.1 apg. and went on to average 7.0 apg. lifetime, which still ranks him twenty-eighth lifetime.

Porter broke into the NBA three years after Van Lier and followed in his footsteps by quickly leading in assists—8.0 in just his third season. He would lead in that department three more times with a peak of 13.4 for the Detroit Pistons in 1978–1979. Porter ended his ten-year career averaging 8.1 apg., which places his average fourteenth in the annals of the NBA. He was also the first player to reach 1,000-plus assists in a season.

The other star out of St. Francis was Maurice Stokes. His story is a tragic one. He lasted only three seasons in the NBA, but he was an All-Star in each of those years. He may not have led the league in assists, but the 6' 7", 240-pound power forward/center could pass the ball well for a big man with an average of 5.3 apg. On two occasions he finished third in the league for assists per game and total assists.

He led the league in rebounding as a rookie (16.3 rpg.) for the Rochester Royals, and compiled career averages of 17.3 rpg. and 16.4 ppg. on route to his Hall of Fame induction. His career ended before the start of the 1958–1959 season as he was struck down by post-traumatic encephalopathy. In the 1957–1958 season finale, he fell to the hardwood, struck his head, and lost consciousness. Three days later, at the age of just twenty-four, he went into a coma and became paralyzed for life. He passed away a few months shy of his thirty-seventh birthday.

WHO WAS RESPONSIBLE FOR THE ORIGIN AND THE SUCCESS OF THE ORIGINAL AIR JORDAN BASKETBALL SHOES, AND HOW HAS THE WORLD OF SNEAKERS EVOLVED OVER THE YEARS?

Long ago kids just *had* to have a pair of P.F. Flyers "canvas shoes"—some youths went with Keds, but TV commercials let kids know that only P.F. Flyers would let them run their fastest and jump their highest thanks to its built-in Magic Wedge, also known as the Action Wedge. The production of those sneakers dates back to 1937 when B.F. Goodrich wanted to assure parents that sneakers—at least *their* sneakers—would not harm children's feet, knees, hips, and/or backs. The initials P and F stood for "posture foundation," referring to a group of orthopedic specialists that B.F. Goodrich hired to design their athletic shoe.

P.F. Flyers is also said to be the first sneaker to use a major sports figure to market a pair of basketball shoes when, in 1958, they signed Boston Celtics star guard Bob Cousy to an endorsement contract.

Actually, the only other major competitor to P.F. Flyers and Keds was Converse, a company that goes back to 1917, further than both of those manufacturers. In fact, their Chuck Taylor All Star shoe had a stranglehold on the world of basketball for years. It was the footwear of Wilt Chamberlain when he turned in his 100-point game in 1962. The "Olympic white" Chuck Taylor was the official sneaker of the US basketball team in the first year that sport debuted in Olympic competition—back in 1936, when, on a muddy outdoor court, the US team took the gold medal in a not-so-rousing 19–8 win over Canada. The Chuck Taylors stayed the official sneaker for the US Olympic teams through the games of 1968.

That sneaker held sway until around the late 1960s. It seems as if for a long period of time no serious young basketball player considered any footgear other than the Chuck Taylors, which were basically canvas shoes with rubber soles.

That is until Nike stuck its foot and footwear in the door in 1972. That's when, as Brendan Bowers of BleacherReport.com puts it, "the shoe industry exploded." Nike came up with its Nike Bruin that year, using leather and suede, not canvas.

Puma leaped into the market with what is believed to be "the first signature sneaker in basketball history" when it came out with its Puma Clyde, a basketball shoe they customized for Walt "Clyde" Frazier in 1973. Beneath the Puma logo on the side of the sneaker was the word *Clyde*, spelled out in gold script.

Other NBA stars had tie-ins with sneaker companies including Julius "Dr. J" Erving, George Gervin, and Moses Malone. But what is considered by many to be "the most iconic basketball shoe in sneaker history" was the Air Jordan I. The shoe, made of leather, had an air pocket in the sole, and it featured the Chicago Bulls' red, black, and white colors.

As for its origin and its originator, credit goes to Nike creative director Peter Moore, the same man who designed the "Jumpman" logo, which, according to Matt Schudel of the *Washington Post*, "helped propel the Jordan brand of shoes and athletic wear into a multibillion-dollar industry."

Moore and another Nike executive named Rob Strasser believed basketball had boundless marketing possibilities and "were instrumental in signing Michael Jordan, then beginning his career with the Chicago Bulls, to a long-term contract with Nike." That deal paid off enormously for both Nike and Jordan. Air Jordan I sneakers went on sale in April 1985, selling for $65, and that was before Jordan had even worn them on an NBA court.

Now, when he *did* wear them, in an exhibition contest, controversy arose. At the time, the NBA mandated that all sneakers be solid white or black (the Celtics were an exception, being permitted to wear green basketball shoes). So, before Jordan could wear his shoes again, the NBA banned them. Nike ran a commercial about the incident, kids clamored to buy the shoes, and sales soared, spurred by the league's decree. Nike actually sent NBA commissioner David Stern a letter of thanks for the publicity, and the league soon lifted the ban.

That's when the Foot Locker shoe franchise upped its order for the sneaker from five thousand pairs to one hundred thousand. Before a year had gone by, the total number of Air Jordans sold eclipsed the million mark. Through the year 2021, "the Jordan brand accounted for more than 10 percent of Nike's annual revenue of $44.5 billion."

For the record, by 2001, Converse was unable to keep up with Nike and Adidas, so it declared bankruptcy. Nike bought Converse for $315 million two years later. By 2015, Nike was selling an average of 270,000 Chuck Taylors per day.

HOW HAVE THE COSTS TO MANUFACTURERS AND CONSUMERS CHANGED OVER THE YEARS REGARDING BASKETBALL SHOES?

The cost of all companies' sneakers has shot up dramatically over the years. A pair of Converse sneakers cost a mere $3.95 in 1957, and a *Los Angeles Times* article from 1988 states that "Flyers sold for less than $15 four decades ago. The new version will cost $60 to $70."

Today a consumer expects to fork over $70 on the low range and possibly $250 for a pair of sneakers, with many young people opting for Nike or Adidas shoes. P.F. Flyers touts their Unisex Center Hi as the sneaker worn in the movie *The Sandlot*, and priced them at around $88 per pair. The above figures don't take into account special basketball shoes—prices fluctuate, but one site lists a pair of size 14 Kobe 9 Elite "Strategy" shoes at close to $5,000.

Interestingly, in 2014, Nike reported that it cost them $28.50 to produce a pair of sneakers with about $27.50 of that amount going for "Chinese factory labor and overhead cost, plus $1 in shipping." With profits abounding, one source stated that Michael Jordan earned $130 million from his Nike shoe label "in the twelve months ended in May 2019."

JUST WHO WAS CHUCK TAYLOR?

While his name is well known in the world of basketball, the man himself isn't. Not many know exactly who he was or what he did. Abraham Aamidor wrote a biography of Taylor, appropriately titled *Chuck Taylor, All Star*. He observes that the situation with Taylor's name on a product "became like Betty Crocker in a sense. If you were a cook, you knew the name Betty Crocker. There was no such person as Betty Crocker. But there really was such a person as Chuck Taylor. Most Americans didn't know that."

Taylor, whose signature began appearing on his Converse All Star sneakers way back in 1932, played semipro basketball, so he knew the game and footgear firsthand. He was born only ten years after the sport of basketball was invented. After playing high school ball in Columbus, Indiana, he wound up playing for the Firestone Non-Skids team in Akron, Ohio. In 1922, he became a salesman for the Converse company, where he played on the firm's team and gave clinics.

A coworker once said about Taylor, "He was a lovable guy and fun to be around and a nice guy, and he, at one point, knew every college basketball coach in the country. And if you wanted to hire a coach, you went through him." He must have been affable—he never requested any royalty payments for his endorsements.

That, despite his name (and the quality of the shoe) clearly selling a heap of sneakers. Aamidor says, "People would order 'Chuck's shoe' or 'Chuck Taylor's shoe' instead of the Converse All Star. So his signature was added just under the five-point star. Brilliant marketing, brilliant branding." Better, it seems, than the benefit of having the Cousy name on Flyers.

Taylor stayed on the job in the mid-1960s after having been basketball's version of Willie Loman in *Death of a Salesman*, except that in Taylor's case his forty-plus years on the road were lucrative ones. It's been said that for many of his years, the nomadic Taylor made hotels his home for 365 days each and every year!

In 1969, he was inducted into the Naismith Memorial Basketball Hall of Fame for his service as an ambassador for the game. Later that year he passed away, leaving behind a lasting legacy.

WHAT NBA PLAYER WORE THE LARGEST SHOE SIZE OF ALL?

Long ago the claim was made that eight-time All-Star center Bob Lanier, who stood 6' 10" and weighed 250 pounds, wore the largest sneakers ever, a boatlike size 22. The Basketball Hall of Fame even displayed a bronzed pair of his sneakers—and that was before he was inducted into the hall.

The claim came under fire in 1989 by Gary Stokan, a representative of the Converse company. He stated, "The 22 he was reputed to wear was a Korean size." Regardless, as Lanier, who is still the Detroit Pistons lifetime leader in scoring with his 22.7 ppg. average, told *HOOP* magazine, "A lot of people can put both feet into one of my shoes."

It's now believed that the 7' 1" 325-pound Shaquille O'Neal wore size-22 sneakers, which had to be custom-made. A size 11 is considered to be on the large size for most men, but O'Neal's shoes dwarf that of the average man.

WHO HOLDS THE SINGLE GAME RECORD FOR SEVERAL OF BASKETBALL'S MAIN STATISTICS: POINTS SCORED, REBOUNDS, ASSISTS, AND BLOCKED SHOTS?

Most fans know that Chamberlain holds the record for the most points in one game with a mind-boggling 100 points (more on this later). He also holds five of the top seven spots for this statistical category. In the 1961–1962 season alone, he had games in which he scored 100 points, 78, and 73 points, plus he drained 67 points twice and hit for 65 another time. Over a period of eight days, he once had three games in which he scored 62 or more points.

Kobe Bryant came up big in 2006 when he fired up 81 points, second-most ever, and David Thompson scored 73 on the final day of the 1977–1978 season for his Denver Nuggets (more on this game later).

Certainly, the way NBA games are played has drastically changed throughout the decades, so some sources list rebound records from the 1983–1984 season separately from older records. Nevertheless, the official record for the most rebounds yanked down in a game is an incredible fifty-five by Chamberlain on November 24, 1960. He has five of the eight highest single-game rebound totals ever. Based on games since the 1983–1984 season, the top rebounder is Charles Oakley with thirty-five in April 1988 when he was with the Chicago Bulls.

As skilled as John Stockton, Rajon Rondo, Jason Kidd, and Kevin Johnson are, the single game assists record holder is Scott Skiles. On the night before New Year's Eve, the Orlando Magic guard dished off the ball for assists 30 times. Stockton owns the next three rungs on this ladder (when based on stats from 1983–1984 onward) with 28, 27, and 26 assists, but Skiles, who averaged 6.5 apg. over his ten NBA seasons, is nevertheless the record holder. His career average ranks forty-third lifetime, but for one magical night, he wore the crown. Prior to Skiles, Kevin Porter of the Nets once had a 29-assists game, and Boston's Bob Cousy enjoyed a game with 28 assists.

Likewise, the king of rejections is Elmore Smith. In 1973, when he was with the Lakers, this seven-footer wasn't to be messed with around the paint—he blocked seventeen shots. He's in the top six for this stat three times with Manute Bol (fifteen blocks twice) and Shaquille O'Neal (fifteen once) for company.

WHO ARE THE SINGLE-SEASON LEADERS FOR THE STATS IN THE ABOVE CATEGORIES?

A list of Chamberlain's records and feats would rival the list Santa checks twice each year. So it's far from surprising that the record holder for the most points scored in an NBA season is Wilt Chamberlain. His statistics and achievements are still as gigantic as the man himself many decades after he played his final game in 1973.

In the 1961–1962 season he amassed 4,029 points, making him the only player to ever top the 4,000-point plateau. He also has the second, fourth, and fifth slots on the all-time list of most points in a season. Therefore, he is responsible for four of the top five season-scoring binges ever. Michael Jordan holds down the third spot with 3,041 points.

Chamberlain is also responsible for the top three averages for rebounds per game played and six of the best seven seasons in that realm. It was a case of total control for the man who averaged more than 27 rpg. for a two-year stretch over his *first two seasons* (1960–1962), with the record of 27.2 rpg. coming in 1960–1961.

John Stockton had a similar monopolistic run. He is the only man to average more than 14 assists per game played and he did that over a two-year period (1989–1991). He set the all-time high in 1989–1990 when he averaged an extraordinary 14.54 dishes per game. He also owns five of the top six best averages in this area with only Isiah Thomas intruding.

As for blocked shots, Mark Eaton averaged 5.56 rejections each time out in 1984–1985. He is followed by Manute Bol (4.96 in 1985–1986) and Elmore Smith (4.85 in 1973–1974).

WHO HAS THE RECORD FOR LEADING THE NBA IN ASSISTS THE MOST SEASONS?

John Stockton. He accomplished this nine times. Leaders in this category often find their dominance runs in streaks. Every one of Stockton's years atop the NBA came in a row from 1987 through the season ending in 1996.

Likewise, the number two man on this list, Bob Cousy, won eight straight assists titles. Oscar Robertson's seven titles came over an eleven-year span. Steve Nash and Jason Kidd led the NBA in dishing off passes for points five times each—Nash over a period of seven seasons and Kidd over six seasons. Finally, Chris Paul led the league five times, but over a longer period of time. He won his first assists title for the 2013–2014 season and his last one in 2021–2022.

WHO ELSE WAS ABLE TO LEAD THE NBA FOR LONG PERIODS OF TIME IN VARIOUS STATISTICAL CATEGORIES?

The top men include points scored per game—Michael Jordan, ten times (over his fifteen NBA seasons); three-point field goals and three-pointers attempted—Stephen Curry, seven in both departments; two-point field goal percentage—Wilt Chamberlain, nine; best three-point field goal percentage—Kyle Korver, four times; free throw percentage—Bill Sharman, seven; free throws made—Karl Malone, eight; total points—Michael Jordan, eleven times; most triple-doubles—Jason Kidd, eleven; best field goal percentage—Shaquille O'Neal, ten.

The list rambles on: offensive rebounds—Moses Malone, eight times; defensive rebounds—Dwight Howard, six; total rebounds and rebounds per game—Chamberlain, eleven; most steals—Chris Paul (who also led for steals per game six times) five; blocked shots—Dikembe Mutombo, five; turnovers—James Harden, six; most games played—A. C. Green, eight times; minutes played—Chamberlain, eight times and nine times for the most minutes played per game.

WHAT IS LEFT TO SAY ABOUT CHAMBERLAIN THAT HASN'T ALREADY BEEN COVERED?

When he hung up his sneakers for the last time at the age of thirty-six, his accomplishments were the stuff of legend. Chamberlain authored forty-nine of the fifty-seven highest point outputs by players in a single game. Think about that. One man turned in 86 percent of the most prolific individual scoring feats ever. With a career average of 30.1 ppg., which was good for 31,419 lifetime points, and with 23,924 rebounds (22.9 rpg.), he was unstoppable, and arguably the greatest offensive weapon ever.

The season he scored 100 points in a single game (1961–1962), he averaged 50.4 points each and every game—no off nights for him. Hard to believe, but in his 100-point game, he even managed to *somehow* make his free throws (using the Granny style), going 28-of-32 from the line (.875). He shot 36-of-63 from the field, including his final finger-roll bucket. He hit that with 45 seconds to play, but chose not to take another shot because he said he just liked the way the round number 100 sounded versus 102.

His quarter-by-quarter point outputs in the 169–147 win were 23, 18, 28, and 31. The Knicks' top three scorers combined for 103 points, while the 76ers' second-leading scorer, Al Attles, was responsible for just 17 points.

"Wilt the Stilt" not only set a record for the most points in a game, he established other records: most free throws made, most field goals attempted and made, most points in a quarter (31), and most points scored in a half with 59. That week, he averaged 73 ppg. in his four games played.

Critics point out that at times he may have been more concerned about his statistics than winning championships, but when it comes to what he accomplished, his numbers just don't lie.

Remember, too, that even though the fourteen-year veteran played in 1,045 regular season games and another 160 in playoff action, averaging 45.8 minutes played over that entire period, he never fouled out of a game.

Trivia items: by the time Chamberlain was a senior at Philadelphia's Overbrook High, more than two hundred colleges were competing for him. One time his Overbrook team defeated Villanova in a scrimmage. Scoring splurges were nothing new to him—in high school he once scored 90 points during a 32-minute game, and that included 60 points coming over a 12-minute barrage. It's rather amazing that Chamberlain's biggest foe, Bill Russell, was gawky in high school and was almost cut from the team, and, unlike his nemesis, received only one scholarship offer, from USF.

WHAT NBA CENTER PROVED THAT BIG MEN COULD BE HIGHLY RELIABLE AT THE FREE THROW LINE?

The best example is Jack Sikma, a 6' 11" center and sometime power forward. He made good on .849 of his career foul shots and led the NBA in that category during the 1987–1988 season when he shot .922 from the line to finish ahead of Larry Bird (.916) in one of Sikma's two seasons to top .900. The only other centers to own a career free throw percentage higher than .830 are Mike Gminski, Bill Laimbeer, Karl-Anthony Towns, and Yao Ming.

Dan Issel, an undersized center/power forward at 6' 9", was no slouch at the line, either. He once strung together sixty-three consecutive foul shots made. Not far behind him was a 7' center who once made sixty straight free throws—Dirk Nowitski.

WHO ARE SOME OF THE MOST NOTABLE FATHER-AND-SON COMBINATIONS TO PLAY IN THE NBA?

The 2022 NBA champion Golden State Warriors alone had four players whose fathers played in the same league. They were Klay Thompson, the son of Mychal; Gary Payton II, whose father Gary once led the league in steals per game; Andrew Wiggins, the 2014–2015 Rookie of the Year, whose father is Mitchell; and Stephen Curry, the son of Dell Curry, a former winner of the Sixth Man Award who is also the father of Seth Curry.

Some of these father-and-son duets were touched upon earlier, such as the Paxson family and Rick Barry along with his offspring. Others not yet mentioned include Kenyon Martin and Kenyon Jr.; Kobe Bryant, whose father was Joe "Jellybean" Bryant. Kobe's uncle Chubby Cox also played in the NBA, albeit for only seven games.

The list continues with the father listed first: Bob and Danny Ferry; Butch and Jan van Breda Kolff; and the Gerald Henderson Sr. and Jr. combo. There is also John Lucas and his son John Lucas III. The father shares the record for the most assists in a quarter, fourteen, with Steve Blake.

Ernie Vandeweghe, who skipped one year of NBA play to attend medical college, is the father of Kiki, a two-time All-Star. There was yet another relative as Kiki's uncle Mel Hutchins also saw NBA action in the 1950s.

Next comes Larry Nance and Nance Jr.; Tim Hardaway and Hardaway Jr.; Tito and Al Horford; Bill and Luke Walton; Henry and Mike Bibby (Henry also happens to be the brother of Major League Baseball pitcher Jim Bibby, who once threw a no-hitter); Doc and Austin Rivers; Ed Manning and Danny; George Mikan and Larry; Dolph Schayes and Danny; and Arvydas and Domantas Sabonis.

The previously mentioned Harvey Grant has three sons, Jerami and Jerian, who made it to the NBA, and Jerai, who has played professionally overseas.

Matt Guokas and his son Matty became the first family to feature both a dad and his son owning NBA championship rings—Matt with the Warriors of Philadelphia, and Matty also with a team from Philly, the 76ers. They also wore the same jersey number, 14. Then there was the Al McGuire and Allie duo—the first such combo to both play for the same team, the Knicks.

Finally, in the 1990–1991 season, a record seven sons of NBA veterans were on various rosters: Rex Chapman (son of Wayne), Sean Higgins (son of Earle), John Paxson, Kiki Vandeweghe, Danny Ferry, Danny Manning, and Danny Schayes. When Schayes was joined by rookie Jon Barry on the 1992–1993 Bucks, it marked the first time sons of Hall of Famers were teammates.

DARRYL DAWKINS BECAME FAMOUS FOR SHATTERING A BACKBOARD WITH A MIGHTY DUNK, BUT WHO WAS THE FIRST NBA PLAYER TO CAUSE SUCH DAMAGE?

The answer is a man who became much more famous for playing on television as an actor as opposed to being a basketball player. It was Chuck Connors, who played the lead role in the show *The Rifleman*. He became a member of the Boston Celtics for their first season in 1946 as a 6' 5" forward/center. He lasted for only one season, scoring 4.5 ppg. He did, however, make an impression when he took a set shot from 15 to 20 feet from the hoop, which bounced off the rim and shattered what had to be a rather flimsy backboard at the Boston Garden.

Never a star, Connors was nevertheless athletic enough to play sixty-seven games in Major League Baseball as a first baseman (who could only muster a lifetime .238 batting average and two home runs).

HOW GOOD ARE/WERE THE HARLEM GLOBETROTTERS?

While the barnstorming Trotters beat up on the hapless Washington Generals at will in lopsided matchups, the outcome of those games was not important. Still, make no mistake, the Harlem squad has always been made up of very talented players.

Over the years, some of the Globetrotters legends have included the genial Meadowlark Lemon, known as the "Clown Prince" of the team; Marques Haynes, who was said to be able to dribble a basketball 348 times in a minute; another dribbling sensation Fred "Curly" Neal, easily recognized by his shaved bald head; Goose Tatum, one of eight Trotters to have his jersey number retired; and "Sweet" Lou Dunbar, who spent twenty-seven years with the Globetrotters.

The Simpsons has an episode in which Krusty the Clown made a ludicrous wager, betting against the Globetrotters and losing a bundle based on his hunch. "I thought the Generals were due," he laments. As Krusty watches the game, he is dumbfounded by the ineptitude of three Generals who are supposedly guarding a Globetrotter just standing in place while spinning the ball on a fingertip. "Just take it! Take the ball," Krusty shouts.

In reality, the team began their hijinks only when they realized they were so dominant they had to inject humor into the games to hold fans' interest. Simply put, the Trotters were very good. As the *Official NBA Basketball Encyclopedia* states, the only reason they originally began to clown around with the ball in 1949 was because they came to realize that "they weren't going to get return engagements by routing local favorites unless they put on a show to dazzle fans. Soon they added tricks to their repertoire of routines such as spinning the ball on their fingers, drop-kicking it toward the goal, and even bouncing it off their heads into the basket. Occasionally, they would line up in a football formation and snap it to [Inman] Jackson for one of his drop-kicks." Total entertainment.

The team was so good, in fact, that in 1940, they won what was called their first World Basketball Championship by defeating the Chicago Bruins of the ABL (which was owned by George Halas).

More impressive was their ability to beat the Minneapolis Lakers in 1948 and 1949. In their first win over the NBA squad, the Globetrotters squeaked by in a 61–59 nail-biter when they hit a basket at the buzzer at Chicago Stadium. It's noteworthy that the win came two years before the first Black player made a debut in the NBA. The game came about because the Globetrotters' owner and coach, Abe Saperstein, and the Lakers general manager, Max Winter, though good friends, were both convinced they had the best team in existence.

The Lakers would win their league's championship for the 1949–1950 season and the following year as well. Stocked with talent such as future Hall of Famers Jim Pollard and George Mikan, a behemoth then at 6' 10" who earned nicknames such as "Mr. Basketball" and "The Monster," the team was an NBA dynamo. Such stars plus the very nature of the game drew almost eighteen thousand fans to the stadium, a superb attendance figure considering no pro hoop game had ever drawn more than nine thousand in Chicago.

Meanwhile, the Globetrotters featured their most recognizable starters in Haynes and Tatum, who, as their center, stood just 6' 3". In the first half, Mikan outscored Tatum 18–0, and helped his Lakers construct a 32–23 lead.

In the second half, the Trotters double-teamed Mikan and decided to fast-break the Lakers out of the building. The moves worked. Mikan was held to six points and the Globetrotters tied the game before the final quarter. Then, with a minute and a half left to play, Harlem played for the last shot. That was possible due to no 24-second clock at the time and to Haynes's stellar, defense-defying, dribbling magic—he is said to have once dribbled for an entire fourth quarter to run out the clock, icing a one-point victory.

With scant seconds left against the Lakers, Haynes passed to Ermer Robinson, who drilled a thirty-footer. Delirious fans went wild.

A year later the Globetrotters again defeated the Lakers, this time by a 49–45 score. However, in the teams' subsequent six rematches, the Lakers won each contest.

Trivia note: the reason the Trotters became a barnstorming team was they were ousted from their original home, the Savoy Ballroom in Chicago, because they weren't drawing enough fans.

HAVE WOMEN OR WHITE PLAYERS EVER JOINED THE GLOBETROTTERS?

In the fall of 2011, a woman who goes by TNT Lister became the first woman on the team since 1993. Another woman, known as Torch George, earned the nickname "Queen of the Crossover."

As for the very first woman on the team, that honor goes to Lynette Woodard. She had been the captain of the US Olympic women's team that won the gold in 1984. A year later she signed her contract with the Globetrotters, making history. She later played in the WNBA, and in 2004, she was inducted into the Basketball Hall of Fame.

The most recent white player on the Harlem roster is Dazzle Kidon, a 5' 11" guard from Poland. When the Globetrotters were touring that country in 2019, the team saw Kidon, who was a world freestyle basketball champion. Impressed with his ball-handling skills during a postgame meet and greet, the Globetrotters soon added him to their roster.

The first three white players on the team were Saperstein, who, in 1926, had founded the team, Harold "Bunny" Levitt, and the first one actually to be signed to a Globetrotters contract, Bob Karstens. He was the man who, according to the *Los Angeles Times*, was the creator of "many of their signature routines such as the pregame 'Magic Circle.'" He also devised the yo-yo basketball and one filled with weights, which caused it to bounce wildly. Karstens said he had no problems in integrating an all-Black team in 1942.

As for Levitt, he set a record back in 1935 by sinking 499 straight foul shots at a Chicago YMCA, using the Granny style of shooting. After his first miss, he sank 371 more free throws in a row—all on the same day. His second streak ended only when, at 3:00 a.m., janitors kicked him out of the gym. His 5' 4" stature didn't deter him from putting on a show, and he spent four and a half seasons with the Globetrotters. He got his nickname "Bunny" from his mother who observed his diminutive size and his quickness.

Levitt said his one memorable failure as a teacher came with Wilt Chamberlain as a pupil. He wasn't able to improve Wilt's foul-shooting ability. Levitt also spent time as a salesman for Converse shoes and he ran basketball clinics for them.

He later instructed players on the art of free throw shooting, working with Bill Sharman, a lifetime .883 free throw shooter in the NBA, and Calvin Murphy, who shot .892 from the line. Sharman set a record by making fifty-five straight foul shots during competition while also making eleven in a row from the field. He led the NBA in free throw percentage a record five seasons in a row.

The 5' 9" Calvin Murphy held the single-season free throw accuracy record (.958) from 1981 until Jose Calderon shot .981 in 2008–2009, the only time he led the NBA in that department. Murphy also once held the record for the most consecutive free throws made with seventy-eight, eighteen more than the previous record set by Rick Barry.

HOW SUCCESSFUL HAVE THE GLOBETROTTERS BEEN, AND HOW FAR HAVE THEY ROAMED OVER THE YEARS?

Statistics on the Globetrotters may not be exactly official, but it's said they have won more than 27,000 games and, surprising to most fans, they dropped 345 decisions. In their first year of existence, their record was 101–6.

The Globetrotters website shares the following information: They played their first game in Hinckley, Illinois—a trip of only 48 miles, so that day they certainly did not trot around the globe—on January 7, 1927. Since then, they have traveled to play in 124 countries on six continents in front of more than 148 million spectators, with their single largest crowd being 75,000 spectators in Berlin's Olympic Stadium, not long after their first international tour took place in 1950.

In 1949, they played a grueling fourteen games in five days during a tour of Alaska. One wonders if that trip caused the players to dread listening to their "Sweet Georgia Brown" theme music. Naturally, the only continent they never toured was Antarctica. Almost 750 men *and* women have donned the team's famous uniform over the years.

Their all-time winning percentage stands at about .987, so, as Krusty the Clown learned, it's not wise to bet against them. Their website claims that their contests "are real basketball games. The Harlem Globetrotters and their opponents both play to win."

HAVE THE GENERALS, WHO ALSO PLAYED UNDER THE NAMES OF THE BOSTON SHAMROCKS, THE ATLANTIC CITY SEAGULLS, AND THE BALTIMORE ROCKETS, EVER KNOCKED OFF THE GLOBETROTTERS?

According to Mike Vaccaro of the *New York Post*, the answer is yes. On January 5, 1971, the Generals ended a 2,495-game losing skid that stretched back fourteen years to a previous upset. Now, *that* is a long, miserable losing streak; and, yes, this long-suffering group of players was the one Vaccaro called a team that "would run around with the Harlem Globetrotters for 40 or 48 minutes. They would endure tricks. They would play the clown . . . They would walk off the court losers. Again. And again. And again." But not always.

ONE LAST GLOBETROTTERS ITEM: WHO WERE THE BIGGEST-NAME PLAYERS NOT MAINLY ASSOCIATED WITH BASKETBALL TO BE ON THE ROSTER?

From time to time this world-famous team, which in 2002 was enshrined in the Naismith Memorial Basketball Hall of Fame, featured players besides their regulars. Wilt Chamberlain, Connie Hawkins, and Nat "Sweetwater" Clifton began their pro careers (for various reasons) with the Globetrotters before moving on to play in the NBA. In Hawkins's case, he first moved on to the ABA before his glory days with the Phoenix Suns. Even though Chamberlain was only with the Globetrotters from 1958 through 1959, the team retired his #13. The three men mentioned here also were inducted into the Basketball Hall of Fame. In 2003, Magic Johnson was signed to an honorary lifetime contract, a symbolic gesture which was to pay him $1 per year.

Along with those stars, the team occasionally signed a few big names from the world of baseball. Baseball Hall of Fame pitcher Bob Gibson, who won 251 big league games, played basketball at Creighton University, so his signing with the Globetrotters was not a gimmick. Actually, Gibson was prepared to play for Indiana University—he was up for a scholarship but, he said, he was informed that the Hoosiers had filled their quota of Black players, so he became the first ever Black player at Creighton. There he averaged 20.2 ppg. over his sixty-three-game college career.

After signing a contract with the St. Louis Cardinals, he suited up for the Globetrotters for their 1957–1958 season. His basketball roommate, Lemon, said, "I thought Bob was a better basketball player than a baseball player. I think Bob could have played with any

NBA team. He was that good." However, when his Cardinals, fearful of Gibson getting injured in basketball action, offered him $4,000 to devote himself exclusively to baseball, Gibson's days on the court came to an end.

Another Hall of Fame pitcher, the 6' 5" Fergie Jenkins, used his 1965–1967 stint with the Globetrotters to stay fit over baseball's winter offseason. He played in the third quarter with his main schtick being giving up a "home run" to Lemon each night. Another St. Louis Cardinals star, Lou Brock, and Willie Horton of the Detroit Tigers also spent some time with the Globetrotters.

EXACTLY HOW DID THE RUSSIAN TEAM ONCE STEAL THE GOLD AWAY FROM THE AMERICAN TEAM?

Going into the Olympic gold-medal game in Munich, Germany, back on September 10, 1972, the US basketball teams owned an unblemished 63–0 record in Olympic play over the years. That was good enough to rack up seven consecutive gold medals. It was also a team led by coach Hank Iba, a defensive-minded coach who Olympian Doug Collins said would not unleash his "thoroughbred athletes who can run, and shoot, and score."

Just four years earlier during the Olympic trials, Iba had cut Pete Maravich, Calvin Murphy, and Rick Mount, a trio which would go on to score a collective average of 109.9 ppg. in the 1968–1969 NCAA season, and all three were Consensus First Team All-Americans.

Unlike some previous US teams that featured celestial stars such as Jerry West and Bill Russell, the 1972 squad, formidable but perhaps not invincible, had lesser stars such as Tom McMillen, Tom Burleson, and Doug Collins. It was the youngest group of players ever to represent the nation, dating back to 1936.

The team struggled against the bigger and more experienced quasi-professional Russian team. USA player Mike Bantom said the Russian "team had [played] hundreds of games together, and the guys were probably 28, 29, 30 years old."

USA trailed by eight with six minutes to go. A late, furious comeback ensued. With just three ticks left on the scoreboard, Collins was viciously undercut on a drive to the hoop, knocked into the basket stanchion. He sank the first of two free throws to tie the game at 49 points apiece.

Just as he was about to begin his second shot, the buzzer went off, but the lead ref did not stop the action. Collins swished his second free throw, and USA held its first lead of the contest at 50–49.

Under the rules of the day, the ball was still live after the foul shot. At that moment, a Russian coach violated a rule by leaving the designated bench area while the ball was in play. He did this when he stomped over to the scorer's table arguing that the buzzer had gone off because his team had called a timeout, *before* Collins's second shot. Regardless, play continued, and the Russians advanced the ball to midcourt before the coach's actions caused a ref to stop play with one second left. The game seemingly was over.

But no. The Soviets again brought up the matter of being denied the timeout they had tried to call. This time, the refs listened and an official ruled the clock should be reset to three seconds with Russia in possession of the ball under their basket. Play on. That ruling was made despite American contentions that no timeout had ever been called, and that the Russian coach's actions merited a technical foul. At any rate, the ball was put in play with a Russian player chucking an attempted pass from near his own foul line. Nothing doing. Time ran out. Again.

Elation swept over the winning American team. But wait. The clock had not been reset to three seconds, a mistake at the scorer's table. And, *once more*, the officials gave the Russians another shot at pulling out a tainted win. A writer from the *New York Times* addressed the issue of why USA's coach Hank Iba didn't protest. "It began to look as if the officials would give the Russians the extra three seconds for as often as it took them to shoot the winning field goal."

That is precisely what took place. A referee ordered McMillen, who had moments earlier effectively blocked the passer's vision, to back off, to give room to the passer—despite the fact that there was no rule requiring the ref to issue such an order, or for McMillen to obey. The pass sailed down the court to Alexander Belov, who was guarded by Kevin Joyce and Robert Forbes.

That did not deter the 6' 8" Belov—reportedly, he simply knocked the two defenders over, caught the ball, and dropped in an easy layup. Outraged American players pounded their fists on the floor in agony and utter disgust, but the 51–50 outcome would, despite later protests, stand.

Replays revealed even more injustices and noncalls by refs wearing blinders. They allowed, or didn't notice, an illegal substitution (the inbounds passer) by the Russian team just prior to the second inbounds play. Furthermore, Belov had actually shoved the two American defenders directly in front of an oblivious official. In addition to that, the inbound passer on the play may have stepped on the endline as he threw. Finally, under existing rules, the three-second lane violation rule went into effect once the ball is handed over to the inbounds passer and Belov was camped in the lane for approximately five seconds.

None of this mattered as a committee denied the USA protest. The committee was made up of members from Cuba, a country ruled by the Communist Party, Poland, Spain, Italy, and Puerto Rico. The referees who worked the debacle of a game were from Brazil and Bulgaria, a socialist republic.

The Russians claimed that the Americans' protest was "prompted by wounded pride." When the proud USA players refused to accept the silver medal, the Russians called it "simply unethical," but the American athletes knew they had rightfully earned the gold.

This, the twentieth Olympiad, was, as *Life* magazine put it, an event which "started in splendor, stopped in blood, and limped to a close in a jumble of anger, disillusion and blame-throwing." The games were marred by an Arab terrorist attack on Israeli athletes, which resulted in the deaths of seventeen people, "a tragic asterisk that always will be attached to the memory of the '72 Games" (*Beckett Basketball Magazine*). The same could almost be said of the ridiculous, almost farcical ending of the Russian "win" over USA.

WHO HOLDS THE RECORD FOR MOST FREE THROWS MADE IN A ROW IN THE NBA AND IN THE WNBA?

Michael Williams of the Minnesota Timberwolves came close to hitting one hundred foul shots in a row, falling just three short. He did that from March 24, 1993, through November 9, 1993. He heads an illustrious list over Jose Calderon (87 in a row), Dirk Nowitzki (82), and Mahmoud Abdul-Rauf (81).

For WNBA play, start with Elena Delle Donne, who made fifty-eight straight foul shots in one season, 2015, when she was with the Chicago Sky. Unfortunately for her, this was one record she would not hold for very long. Just five weeks later, DeWanna Bonner of the Phoenix Mercury snatched that record when she sank her fifty-ninth foul shot in a row. Uncharacteristically, she missed her next two free throws.

The overall WNBA mark for the most consecutive free throws made stretched across two seasons, 1999–2000, and that streak of sixty-six belongs to Eva Nemcova of the Cleveland Rockers. According to SportsADay.com, she missed her first free throw attempt of the 1999 season, never missed again that year, made her first four attempts the next season, then finally missed while shooting a technical foul, one week shy of the one-year anniversary of the start of her streak. No fluke, Nemcova shot .897 from the line over her five WNBA seasons. Her free throw percentage in 1999 was .894 (62-of-63 shooting), but the recognized leader in this realm is Becky Hammon of the San Antonio Stars, who didn't miss a foul shot in 2014, although she shot just thirty-five free throws.

Delle Donne, by the way, ranks as the most accurate free throw shooter ever for a WNBA career. She's not done yet, but her lifetime percentage from the charity stripe through 2021–2022 is .9372, which is about 3 percent better than the NBA's best, Stephen Curry.

WHO WON THE NBA'S FIRST THREE-POINT CONTEST?

Larry Bird took home $10,000 for ten minutes of work back in 1986. The actual name for the event was "Long Distance Shootout." The 1986 competition was made famous by Bird's braggadocio and his gamesmanship. When informed that an opponent, Leon Wood, had sunk 28 of 31 practice shots the day before the contest, he knew what he was going to do—play some mind games. Shortly before the shootout, Bird strutted into the players' dressing room, gazed at his seven opponents, and asked, "Which one of you guys is going to finish second?"

He also got into Wood's head by telling him he had watched him shooting and he believed that his "shot looks a little different to me." Perhaps too conscious of what should have been an automatic, routine act, Wood was eliminated in the first round. Bird would go on to win the contest again in the following two seasons.

In 1988, when Bird won his third successive three-point contest, he did so in typical swaggering manner—without bothering to remove his warm-up jacket. It seems apt that the man who loved to launch treys wore a jersey with two 3s, making his #33 feared by opponents.

The only other sharpshooter to win this event three times was Chicago's Craig Hodges (all in a row, 1990 through 1992). Others who won the contest twice are Cavs guard Mark Price, Jeff Hornacek of the Jazz, Peja Stojakovic of the Kings, Toronto's Jason Kapono, and Stephen Curry.

Trivia note: in 2022, Minnesota's 6' 11" center, Karl-Anthony Towns, won the three-point contest with the highest score ever in the final round, 29. The odds of him winning were 13-to-1, but he became the second-tallest man to win this event—Dirk Nowitzki, at 7', won it in 2006.

WHAT ARE SOME OF THE HIGHLIGHTS OF SLAM DUNK COMPETITIONS?

This event has been a fan favorite at All-Star games since it began in 1984—although the NBA did feature a dunk contest in 1976–1977 that ran for the entire season. However, the true origin of the contest dates back to the ABA and the first ever competition held in Denver at halftime during their All-Star Game in 1976. It was then that Julius Erving made fans bolt out of their seats with his gravity-defying dunks. His most famous slam took place after he took nearly a full-court dash before leaping to the sky like a jet on its takeoff. Dr. J soared the 15 feet to the hoop to complete his flight with a mighty dunk.

Contrary to a misconception, he did not actually take off from *behind* the foul line, as one foot was on the line. So his trip was just a matter of inches shy of 15 feet, but considering he was not in a cockpit and not propelled by anything but his own power, that distance compares favorably to the famous solo flight of Orville Wright, which went 180 feet. For winning the contest and creating an indelible basketball memory, Erving won a paltry $50 gift certificate.

That All-Star Game was the ninth and final one for the league and it featured a very different format than those held in the NBA. The ABA showcase game pitted the Denver Nuggets who sat atop the seven-team league at the break, versus the All-Stars from all other teams. The Nuggets won the game, rolled on to top the final standings by five games, but lost in the championship series to Erving's Nets.

Returning to dunk highlights, another shining one came when Michael Jordan seemed to float in midair in 1988 after racing from one baseline to the foul line near the other baseline. Flying à la Erving, "His Airness" earned a perfect score with this dunk in the final round to win the event.

Three years later, Boston's Dee Brown theatrically pumped up his Reebok Pumps sneakers and covered his eyes to slam the ball blindly in winning the 1991 NBA Slam Dunk Contest. His high-tops were designed to give strong ankle support when pumped up, and kids flocked their way to stores to emulate Brown.

Gimmicks and props have become popular during the contest and examples such as Dwight Howard donning a Superman cape then taking off, up, up, and away to win the 2008 competition are plentiful. He also once slapped a sticker close to the top of the backboard (at 12 feet, 6 inches) while dunking.

Then there was Serge Ibaka, who seized a teddy bear, which sat on the rim, by using his teeth before slamming the ball. Blake Griffin jumped over the hood of a car for a dunk. JaVale McGee's prop was a second basketball as he dunked two balls in two different adjoining rims almost simultaneously.

Gerald Green jumped over a table one year and another year he dunked while he blew out a candle atop a cupcake that had been placed on the rear of the bucket where it's attached to the backboard. Another time he had Rashad McCants perched on a ladder, holding a ball out for Green to snatch then throw down a windmill dunk from high up in the atmosphere.

Of course, nobody who ever witnessed the time the contest was won by a man who was listed at 5' 6" and 133 pounds will ever forget that astonishing feat. The man was Spud Webb, who despite his lack of height and the fact that he was a fourth-round draft pick (87th overall), spent a dozen seasons in the NBA. He averaged 5.3 apg., but will be forever remembered for winning the Slam Dunk Contest on February 8, 1986, beating out Atlanta teammate Dominique Wilkins, who stood 6' 8" and who was quite the spectacle when it came to dazzling dunks—remember, he wasn't nicknamed "The Human Highlight Film" for nothing.

Vince Carter has his own glistening highlights, including in 2000 when he dunked, sticking his arm into the rim then hanging with his arm up to the elbow on that rim for some time before returning to earth. FranchiseSports.co.uk called his twirling, reverse, 360 windmill slam, his "signature elbow dunk" and his other dunks that day "the greatest individual performance in Slam Dunk Contest history."

To keep this list short, instead of describing other impressive dunks, check out video on the 2016 contest with eyes wide open to witness and appreciate the skill and dramatics of Aaron Gordon and Zach LaVine.

WHO ARE SOME OF THE SHORTEST MEN TO PLAY IN THE NBA?

In addition to Webb, there was another 5' 6" NBA player, but this one, Mel Hirsch, lasted only one season (just thirteen games), 1946–1947. He held the record alone for being the shortest player until Webb came along in 1985.

One inch shorter than Webb, Earl Boykins entered the league in 1999. He played through 2012 and once averaged 15.2 ppg. Like Webb, he was not signed as a publicity stunt, although he did go undrafted. Originally, he became a New Jersey Net as a free agent.

As for the shortest NBA player of them all, that man is Muggsy Bogues. He was listed at 5' 3", and while he never dunked in a regulation game, he said he could manage that feat with relative ease thanks to his 44-inch vertical leap. NBA scouts were well aware of the prowess of this Wake Forest star, whose real first name is Tyrone. The Washington Bullets gobbled him up as the twelfth overall pick in the 1987 NBA Draft. He, too, was the real deal, darting though the tall timber of the league to dish out 7.6 apg., which ranks him nineteenth lifetime. At the line, where a lack of height is inconsequential, he was successful on 83 percent of his shots, a rate quite better than the league norm most any season.

WHAT WAS THE LOWEST-SCORING GAME IN NBA HISTORY?

Back on November 22, 1950, the most boring game ever in NBA play took place with the Fort Wayne Pistons taking on the Minneapolis Lakers. The game was held on the home court of the Lakers, which was smaller than the standard size. To minimize the effectiveness of Lakers giant George Mikan, the Pistons strategy was to freeze the ball. With no shot clock then, the first quarter ended with Fort Wayne on top, 8–7. The Lakers went ahead, 13–11, at the half, and led 17–16 after three quarters. Fans booed, but nothing changed.

By the midway mark of the fourth quarter, both teams had made just one free throw. The Pistons chose to play for the last, potentially game-winning shot when there was still four minutes to go. Rookie Larry Foust hit a hook shot and the Pistons wound up with a tedious, infuriating 19–18 win.

Mikan scored 15 of his team's 18 points, and no other player had more than 5 points. A lousy display of 37 total points made it clear that something had to change, but it took the league three more seasons to figure out that a 24-second clock would revolutionize the game.

WHAT WAS THE TIGHTEST RACE BETWEEN TWO MEN BATTLING DOWN THE STRETCH TO WIN THE SCORING TITLE FOR A SEASON?

Going into the final day of the 1977–1978 season, two scoring machines and future Hall of Famers, San Antonio's George Gervin and Denver's David Thompson, were headed for a photo finish in the race to take the scoring title. The *New York Times* called the outcome "the most remarkable finish in NBA history."

That finish featured the 6' 7" Gervin winning the first of his four scoring titles, but not before an epic Wild West shootout. Both he and Thompson made their debuts in the ABA and both were in just their second NBA season.

On April 9, 1978, Thompson knew he trailed Gervin by two-tenths of a point going into his afternoon season finale against the Pistons. Determined to catch and pass his rival, Thompson went on a shooting spree. He scored the third-highest number of points, a colossal 73, ever in NBA play.

"They got the ball to me, and I was hitting," he said. "Everything was going in for me in the first half. I couldn't keep up with the pace in the second half though. I got a little tired." Indeed, he sank his first eight shots before another one was blocked. Undaunted, he reeled off twelve more in a row, scorching the stat sheet with his 20-of-23 first half shooting, good for 53 points.

Seven hours later, Gervin faced the Jazz fully aware that he needed to pound down 58 points to wrest scoring honors from the man known as "Skywalker." "They kept a hand in my face all night," Gervin recalled. "I was pressing early and I didn't have my rhythm, but I got it after seven or eight minutes. After I got the points that I needed, I asked to come out because I was a little tired and wanted to catch my breath."

That welcome break came a mere minute and a half into the second half with 59 points in the books. In the second period alone he scored 33 points to set a new record for one quarter. The previous record setter? Well, that was Thompson, set earlier that day. Overall, Gervin played 33 minutes in a 153–132 loss, but the title was his.

It took a calculator to determine the scoring champ, and the players' averages had to be carried out two decimal points to do so, a first for NBA competition. When the dust had settled, Gervin outlasted Thompson by a microscopic margin of 27.22 to 27.15 ppg.

WHO IS THE ONLY MAN TO WIN AN NCAA MEN'S NATIONAL TITLE IN HIS FIRST YEAR AS HEAD COACH?

The answer is Steve Fisher—sort of. The explanation: in 1989, veteran Michigan coach Bill Frieder guided his Wolverines to a regular season record of 24–7 and a number three seed in the NCAA Tournament. Then came the wrinkle. He had already received an offer to become the head coach at Arizona State for the following season. When Michigan athletic director Bo Schembechler discovered that, he requested Frieder vacate his job with the Wolverines. Steve Fisher then took over the job as the school's interim coach, and his team rattled off six straight wins, including an 83–81 squeaker over Illinois and an 80–79 overtime win against Seton Hall to claim the NCAA title. It remains their only basketball championship.

Fisher then had the word "interim" erased from his title and went on to lead Michigan to back-to-back Final Fours in 1992 and '93, although those appearances were later vacated.

HOW DIFFICULT IS IT TO BE A MEMBER OF THE 50-40-90 CLUB, MEANING THAT A PLAYER SHOT 50 PERCENT OR BETTER FROM THE FIELD, 40 PERCENT OR HIGHER FROM BEYOND THE ARC, AND 90 PERCENT OR BETTER FROM THE FOUL LINE IN A GIVEN SEASON?

In the 1988–1989 season, Magic Johnson did something only Larry Bird had ever before achieved, shooting better than 50 percent from the field and more than 90 percent from the line. Magic, who shot .509 from the field, made his foul shots at a 91.1 percent clip to lead the league for his only time in that department. As laudable as that was, Johnson only shot .314 from long range.

Bird did him one better a year earlier, becoming the charter member of the 50-40-90 Club, which began in 1986–1987. Bird was later joined by Mark Price, Reggie Miller, Steve Nash (who did this four times), Dirk Nowitzki, Kevin Durant, Stephen Curry, Malcom Brogdon, and Kyrie Irving.

WHO WAS THE FIRST 7' TALL BASKETBALL PLAYER IN NBA HISTORY?

Ralph Siewert. This man stood 7' 1" and played for the St. Louis Bombers and the Toronto Huskies in the NBA's first season (1946–1947). Predictably nicknamed "Sky" and "Timber," he scored just 20 points over his twenty-one games, somehow shooting just 6-for-44 (.136)—little wonder his career was so fleeting. In high school baseball he had been quite a target as his team's first baseman.

In a related note about height, in a recent *Sports Illustrated* article, Pablo S. Torre figured there were probably fewer than seventy American men between the ages of twenty and forty who stood 7' or taller. During the 2021–2022 season, the NBA featured thirteen players from the United States who went 7' or taller. That meant, in theory, that there was an 18 percent chance that an American of that height and in that age range would play in the NBA. Perhaps that's not a scientific conclusion, but it demonstrates how important height is at the pro level, and it supports former Utah Jazz coach Frank Layden's famous saying, "You can't teach height."

Forbes magazine was another source that focused on the importance of height, noting that "more than 42 U.S.-born players listed at 7 feet did debut in NBA games between 1993 and 2013."

WHO ARE THE ONLY PLAYERS TO AVERAGE A TRIPLE-DOUBLE FOR AN ENTIRE SEASON?

For an eon only one man, 6' 5" premier point guard Oscar Robertson, held that distinction. In 1961–1962, his points, rebounds, and assists totals were 30.8, 12.5 (a brilliant average for rebounds by a guard), and 11.4—and he was only in his second pro season. He nearly repeated his terrific feat the next two years, once falling short in assists at 9.5, and the other time with 31.4 ppg., 11.0 apg., and an oh-so-close 9.9 rpg.—just seven more rebounds over the entire season and he would've hit 10.0 on the nose.

During his rookie season he almost achieved the triple-double feat. He averaged 30.5 ppg., 10.1 rpg., and narrowly missed his goal with 9.7 apg., which was the best average ever for a rookie (since topped by Mark Jackson at 10.6 in 1987–1988). "The Big O" fell just twenty total assists shy of reaching triple-double status.

Fifty-five years after Robertson spun his legerdemain on the court, Oklahoma City's point guard Russell Westbrook came along and turned this trick three seasons in a row and four times overall during a fabulous five-year stretch. He led the league in assists in three of those seasons and in scoring once, in 2016–2017 at 31.6 ppg. In that MVP season he also broke Robertson's single-season record for the most triple-double games with forty-two, one more than Robertson. Basketball-Reference.com notes that Westbrook's four seasons with four hundred or more rebounds is the most ever in the NBA by a player who goes 6' 3" or shorter.

Trivia note: Robertson won the NCAA scoring title in all three of his varsity seasons at the University of Cincinnati where he took the Bearcats to two Final Fours. There he averaged 33.8 ppg., which remains the third-highest average in college history, trailing only Pete Maravich and Austin Carr.

Then, over Robertson's first five NBA seasons, he averaged a triple-double with 30.3 ppg. to go with exactly 10.3 rebounds and assists each night. From 1960 to 1968, he was the only player to break the MVP monopoly held by Chamberlain and Russell. Finally, over Robertson's fourteen-year career, his triple-double stats were 25.7 ppg., 9.5 apg., and 7.5 rpg.

WHAT MEN HAVE BEEN ABLE TO RECORD A QUADRUPLE-DOUBLE (OR BETTER)?

According to BasketballNoise.com, Chamberlain once turned in a game with double digits in not four but five categories, meaning he turned in a quintuple-double with 53 points, 32 rebounds, 14 assists, 11 steals, and 24 blocked shots. Keep in mind, blocks did not become an official stat until the 1973–1974 season, and Chamberlain played in his final game at the end of the previous season. More to the point, his quintuple-double game supposedly came in 1968. Controversy remains about the validity and reliability of his stats from that game.

The website reports that others to achieve the quadruple feat are Nate Thurmond (22 points, 14 boards, 13 assists, and 12 blocked shots); Alvin Roberston, the only man on this list with steals as one of his four double-digit categories (20 points, 11 rebounds, 10 assists, and 10 steals for this shooting guard); Hakeem Olajuwon, who did this twice with his best effort being 20 points, 18 rebounds, 10 assists, and 10 blocks; and David Robinson (34 points scored and precisely 10 boards, assists, and blocked shots).

WHO ARE SOME OF THE MEN WHO HAVE PLAYED BOTH PROFESSIONAL BASEBALL AND BASKETBALL?

Start with Dave DeBusschere. He had a 40–21 record in the minors, and in the Majors with the Chicago White Sox he won three games and posted a 2.90 ERA over thirty-six games. Not bad, but in the NBA, he won two championships and became a Hall of Famer. He also served as the commissioner of the ABA and the general manager of the New York Nets and Knicks.

Danny Ainge, who was the first high school player ever to be named an All-American in baseball, football (Notre Dame wanted him as a receiver), and basketball, is also on this list. He came from good stock as his father was a star in three sports and played his college football at the University of Oregon as a teammate of future USC coach John Robinson.

Danny took his Eugene (Oregon) High School team to state championships in 1976 and 1977. As a senior at Brigham Young University, he was named the best college player in the nation, taking home the Wooden Award. Ultimately, he made the right choice when he left his Toronto Blue Jays and became a Boston Celtic. With them, he became an All-Star and won two NBA titles.

Other men on this two-sport list include Ron Reed; Steve Hamilton; Frank Baumholtz; Dick Ricketts; Howie Schultz; Cotton

Nash; Mark Hendrickson; Gene Conley; baseball Hall of Famer Lou Boudreau; Dick Groat, winner of the 1960 National League MVP Award; and the previously mentioned Chuck Connors.

The Naismith Basketball Hall of Fame has featured sports figures from outside the world of the NBA who were basketball standouts, including baseball Hall of Famers Hank Greenberg, Jackie Robinson, and even broadcaster Curt Gowdy.

Because the question mentioned professional baseball and did not specify the Major League level, Michael Jordan qualifies here. Aside from his unmatched NBA play, Jordan spent one season at the AA level as a thirty-one-year-old outfielder for a Chicago White Sox farm club, the Birmingham Barons. In 1994, playing for manager Terry Francona, Jordan proved how difficult it is to hit a round ball squarely with a round bat, striking out 114 times while hitting just .202 with three home runs over 497 plate appearances.

His ineffectiveness reminded observers of a comment made about Joe DiMaggio, a baseball star whose marriage to movie star/ sex symbol Marilyn Monroe failed: "No man can excel at two national pastimes."

WHO HAVE BEEN SOME OF THE HEAVIEST OR BULKIEST-LOOKING PLAYERS IN NBA HISTORY?

Some background first: in 1952, the average weight of NBA players was in the lower 190-pound range. It wasn't until the first decade of the twenty-first century that the average was above 200 pounds. The average hit its all-time high of 221 pounds in 2011. Since then, the average has dipped a bit to 214 in 2021–2022, as the pro game began to seek out faster, more muscular, and very athletic players.

Some hand-selected men noted for their girth include Mel Turpin, who earned the previously mentioned nickname "Dinner Bell Mel" when he was listed at 240 pounds, but that claim shaved a ton of avoirdupois off his true weight. He was sometimes also called "El Mucho Grande" and "Mealman." In the 1984 NBA Draft, Turpin was so coveted that the only men picked ahead of him were Hakeem Olajuwon, Sam Bowie (like Turpin, out of the University of Kentucky), Michael Jordan, Sam Perkins, and Charles Barkley. Turpin lasted 361 games over a period of five NBA seasons, averaged 8.5 points per game, and just 4.6 rebounds per game. A far cry from when he was a Consensus All-American.

Kevin Duckworth, one of only two NBA players out of Eastern Illinois University, was a seven-footer who was listed at 275 pounds, but more realistic reports say he was a lot closer to 300 pounds.

Then there was the previously mentioned Robert "Tractor" Taylor, who carried at least 284 pounds on his 6' 8" frame. Like Duckworth, many sources report he weighed in excess of 300 pounds. He won the MVP of the 1997 National Invitation Tournament when his Michigan Wolverines won that tourney, but he washed out in NBA action—seven seasons with just seventy-three games started and 4.8 ppg. along with 3.7 rpg.

Perhaps the 6' 8" Charles Barkley wasn't exactly fat, but to many he seemed a bit chunky and he became known as the "Mound Round of Rebound" because of his hulking appearance and his proficiency on the boards.

However, the all-time prince of pounds is said to be Oliver Miller, who fought a personal battle of the bulge, checking in at 375 pounds on his massive 6' 9" frame. Others who are in, or nearly in Miller's neighborhood include 7' Shaquille O'Neal, who topped out at 348 pounds; and Sim Bhullar, the first NBA player of Indian descent, is the sixth-tallest player in league history at 7' 5", punishing the scales with his 360 pounds.

Players' weights fluctuate over their careers, but the following men certainly deserve mention for their size:

1. Eddy Curry—one report says when he reached around 400 pounds, he "abandoned his career because his weight wouldn't let him perform."
2. Michael Sweetney, who was drafted by the Knicks in 2003 when he weighed 260 pounds, but was up to 348 just a few years later, according to several sources.
3. Priest Lauderdale stood 7' 4" and weighed 325 pounds, which led to his lasting only two NBA seasons (1.9 rpg. and 3.4 ppg.).

WHAT IS THE AVERAGE HEIGHT OF AN NBA PLAYER?

The average height has, of course, evolved over the history of the NBA. Going back to 1952, on average an NBA player stood 6' 4", hardly someone to gawk at. Flash-forward to the 2021–2022 season, and the average height (while barefooted) had shot up to 6' 6"— eight and a half inches taller than that of the average American male, but down a bit from the peak of 6' 7" in 1987.

The folks at HoopsGeek.com break down players' heights by position, using measurements from when they are in uniform, including their sneakers. Lately, point guards go 6' 2" and shooting guards stand 6' 5". Power forwards check in at a bit over 6' 8" while 6' 6" is about the norm for small/forwards. Finally, the big men—the average center comes in at about two inches under 7'.

To answer the question of which players, based on their height, get the most playing time, HoopsGeek.com features a chart that explores this issue. While the chart doesn't produce a perfect bell-shaped curve, it comes pretty close. The 6' 4" to 6' 8" range of players represents the men who see the most action, more than 50 percent of all the minutes played in 2021–2022. Meanwhile, the extremes of the shortest and tallest players reveal much less playing time. That makes sense because that season there were only twenty-one players who measured 6' or less, and just twenty-nine who stood more than 7'.

WHICH BASKETBALL PLAYERS HAD INTERESTING OR UNUSUAL IDIOSYNCRASIES OR MANNERISMS AT THE FREE THROW LINE?

Hall of Fame guard Hal Greer shot jumpers for his free throws, and his logic was basically, "I'm practicing my jumpers when I shoot free throws, and sort of working on my foul shots with my jumpers from the field."

BleacherReport.com states that Anthony Mason "dribbled a few times, held the ball up in his hands as if to release, then spent the remaining three-to-four seconds with the ball perched and paused like an annoying video game glitch." Lane violations were not uncommon with him at the line. Karl Malone spun the ball in the air near his body, seemed to whisper something softly, hesitated much like Mason, and then and only then did he release the basketball.

Adrian Dantley caressed the ball, turning it over in his hands a few times as if to inspect its surface, before taking his free throw. Moses Malone used to lift his trademark goggles up so they sat on his forehead before taking aim and shooting foul shots.

Nick Van Exel felt more comfortable shooting not from just behind the line, but from a few steps behind the line. Chamberlain tried this method, too, along with other experiments from the line such as a "variation on the hook shot" and the Granny style shot, but none worked.

Gilbert Arenas wrapped the basketball around his waist three times before he would shoot. Richard Hamilton's ritual was described by BleacherReport.com like this: "First, 'Rip' takes a deep breath, takes two dribbles in front (one on the side) and lets fly a dagger."

Jeff Hornacek had his own ritual. Before each foul shot, he would rub his cheek as a tribute to his children who must've been pleased when they saw him do this on television. Similarly, Jason Kidd honored his wife and kids by blowing a kiss before flipping free throws.

WHAT PLAYERS HAD OTHER NOTEWORTHY HABITS OR MANNERISMS?

Kevin Garnett and later LeBron James had the pregame habit of throwing chalk into the air then clapping their hands. Michael Jordan did something along those same lines when he was with the Bulls and Johnny "Red" Kerr was broadcasting games. Jordan would put rosin on his hands, stand near Kerr, then clap his hands so that Kerr would get a dusting.

Pete Maravich was known for the floppy socks he wore. Dick Barnett had an unusual jump shot—at the top of his leap he kicked his legs up high, as if he was trying to kick his own butt. He was sometimes called "Fall Back Baby" due to his unusual form.

Tim Duncan always liked to hang from the rim just before the PA announcer introduced him before the start of games. Garnett and Vince Carter did likewise, and Dwyane Wade would hang from the rim but add his own touch by doing three pullups over the rim.

WHO ARE SOME OF THE PEOPLE WHO WERE SO SUCCESSFUL AND RESPECTED AT THEIR COLLEGES THAT A COURT OR THE STADIUM WAS NAMED IN THEIR HONOR?

Coach K court, an homage to Mike Krzyzewski, is located inside Cameron Indoor Stadium in Durham, North Carolina, and is home to the Duke Blue Devils. The school named both the venue and the actual hardwood court after two Duke legends. The building's name pays tribute to Eddie Cameron, who coached football at the school from 1942 through 1945 when their head coach was serving in World War II. Over those four years he won three Southern Conference titles and came up with a Sugar Bowl win over Alabama. Later, he was a founder of the Atlantic Coast Conference. But Cameron's big claim to fame was impressively racking up 226 basketball wins, making him the second-winningest Duke hoops coach ever (albeit almost a thousand victories shy of Coach K).

Naturally, no thoughts were given to changing the name of Duke's venerable facility—a name it had since 1972—so to honor Krzyzewski, the court was named after him in November 2000 during a postgame ceremony. He retired in 2022 with 1,202 career wins. Only he and Syracuse coach Jim Boeheim are Division I coaches with a thousand or more wins.

Syracuse named its court after Boeheim, who, upon his retirement in early 2023, won 1,116 games, all with the same team. A large rendition of his signature is prominently located under the orange S at midcourt.

Coach Dean Smith led the UNC basketball program from 1961 through to the 1996–1997 season, retiring as the winningest college coach ever. To many, he *was* UNC basketball. That's why the arena in which the Tar Heels have played their home games since January 18, 1986 (fittingly against Duke), is known as the Dean Dome. Well, it's called that by most fans, but its actual title is the Dean E. Smith Student Activities Center.

The school paid tribute to another of their successful coaches when, in 2018, they named the playing area after Roy Williams, who was then their head basketball coach. The UNC alum retired from his coaching duties in 2021 with 903 wins to his credit.

Rupp Arena in Lexington, Kentucky, got its name to honor the Kentucky Wildcats coach of forty-one years. His career dates back to 1930, and in 1972 he won his final game, his 876th victory—once the highest total ever and, through 2021–2022, still seventh all-time. It took a quarter of a century before Dean Smith usurped Rupp.

John Wooden is, overwhelmingly, the owner of the most NCAA championships ever with ten. His is an interesting tale of how schools—plural—have honored him. His home venue when he was at UCLA was Pauley Pavilion, and it was already named after Edwin W. Pauley, who was a University of California Regent and had donated almost 20 percent of the total cost of constructing the building, which ran a bit over $5 million.

Incidentally, and by way of comparison, a Duke benefactor and alum named David Rubenstein donated $10 million to Duke athletics during a campaign. Now the Rubenstein Pavilion is a welcome addition to Cameron Indoor Stadium.

At any rate, UCLA named the Bruins' basketball court after John and his late wife, Nell, in 2003. The burning question is why they waited so long to do this. Wooden, then ninety-three years old, had been retired from coaching for twenty-eight years after guiding UCLA to 620 wins from 1948 to 1975 (he also won 59 while coaching Indiana State to begin his career). After he hung up his clipboard, the Bruins have managed to win only one more title (in 1995).

In 2008, Indiana State named its basketball floor inside Hulman Center after Wooden (who had recently celebrated his ninety-eighth birthday) and his wife. Wooden had served as the school's basketball coach, athletics director, and baseball coach for his two-year stint there.

Not only that, he was the first person to be inducted into the basketball Hall of Fame as a player *and* as a coach. He was a guard for the Purdue Boilermakers when they won it all in 1932. Remember, with UCLA he once set a record with an unfathomable winning streak of eighty-eight games, and he engineered four 30–0 seasons.

Louisiana State University chose to honor one of their greatest players and their most electrifying showman ever by naming an arena (their LSU Assembly Center) the Pete Maravich Assembly Center in Baton Rouge, Louisiana. They bestowed that honor in 1988, not long after he passed away. They didn't pay tribute to him earlier because under Louisiana law, no state-owned building is permitted to be named after someone who is still alive. They could have named the facility the "House That Pete Built" because the Tigers' program had long taken a backseat to the school's football program until Maravich's mesmerizing play led to LSU building a bigger home facility. Some locals refer to the arena as Pete's Palace.

Returning to the coaching ranks, other select coaches to have a court named after them include Eddie Sutton at Oklahoma State; Nolan Richardson of Arkansas; head coach John Thompson is honored at Georgetown; the University of Florida's Billy Donovan; Lute Olson and his late wife, Bobbi, at Arizona; Allen Fieldhouse in Lawrence, Kansas, is named for KU's great coach Phog Allen; Louisville pays tribute to coach Denny Crum; and the Runnin' Rebels of UNLV play home games on Jerry Tarkanian Court.

Lou Henson was recognized at Illinois; likewise, Bobby Cremins at Georgia Tech; Gene Keady at Purdue; Maryland's court is named for Gary Williams; and the Crisler Center in Ann Arbor, Michigan, home of the Michigan Wolverines, honors a man who didn't coach basketball but who served as the university's head football coach and athletic director, Herbert "Fritz" Crisler.

Finally, North Carolina State managed to honor William Neal Reynolds while also honoring their famous coach, Jim Valvano, in naming their coliseum. So the James T. Valvano Arena at William Neal Reynolds Coliseum is now the facility's lengthy name. It should be pointed out, though, that the Wolfpack's home court for men's basketball is now PNC Arena, located off campus.

HOW ABOUT WOMEN'S COACHES TO RECEIVE HONORS LIKE THE MEN MENTIONED ABOVE?

Arguably the biggest name in the world of NCAA Women's basketball is still Pat Summitt, even though in 2020, Stanford's Tara VanDerveer climbed over Summitt's record for career wins in women's Division I play. Summitt won 1,098 games over thirty-eight seasons, not counting her victories as the United States' Olympics gold medal–winning coach. She also won eight NCAA Division I championships. So it was no wonder that the college she coached for her entire career, the University of Tennessee, named their court after her (they also erected a statue of her on their campus).

The Lady Volunteers head coach was a living legend, never once posting a losing season and having never missed playing in the NCAA Tournament. In 2000, she was named the Naismith Basketball Coach of the Century, and SportingNews.com rated her as the eleventh greatest coach of all time in *any* sport. She is a member of three prestigious halls of fame, including one for her playing prowess.

In 2005, when she won her 880th game to break the then existing record for most wins by a Division I coach held by Dean Smith, it was announced that the court was to be named the Summitt, a very fitting name. With a lifetime winning percentage of .841, she clearly deserves the recognition.

The second and third coaches of women's basketball to be similarly honored were Kay Yow of North Carolina State and Gary Blair, the head coach of the Texas A&M Aggies since 2003 and winner of 852 career games through 2021–2022. Yow led the Wolfpack from 1975 to 2009 and won 737 games.

HUSTLE AND SCRAPPINESS ARE CONSIDERED TO BE TWO FINE ATTRIBUTES FOR BASKETBALL PLAYERS, BUT HOW CAN SUCH TRAITS BE OVERDONE?

Larry Bird's willingness to sacrifice his body eventually took its toll on the Celtics legend. He threw himself on the court for loose balls even while suffering from a bad back that would make most people unable to walk without a cane, let alone run and dive to the hardwood floor. There's no doubt his subsequent health issues curtailed his career. His 1988–1989 season, his tenth in the league, was limited to six games. That was the first time he appeared in fewer than seventy-four contests. Not counting that season, he never scored less than 20.2 ppg. and that came in his final season, when he surely realized it was time to make his departure.

Hall of Fame center Nate Thurmond said of Cleveland Cavaliers guard Mark Price, "He's an outstanding guard. The only criticism I have is he plays with *too* much enthusiasm. Don't throw yourself up against a piece of wood—the floor is going to win," he chuckled. He went on to say players such as Price are too valuable to teams for them to risk an unnecessary injury. Thurmond compared Price to Bird, believing the Celtic great "lost a year or two off his career by throwing his body to the floor too much.

"All-out hustle, especially when you first come into the league, is fine, but Price must make up his mind sometimes, 'I can't get to that ball.'"

SPEAKING OF BIRD, JUST HOW FOCUSED WAS HE?

When it came to, say, shooting the ball, Bird was a picture of total concentration. A classic example: in one game as he stepped to the free throw line a disturbance broke out in the crowd. The referee asked him if he wanted to wait for the fans to settle down. Bird gazed up at the spectators and saw several young men waving full-length posters of bikini-clad models at Bird. Instead of being distracted, he grinned, took the ball, and drained his free throws.

He led the NBA in foul shooting accuracy four times, connected on 88.6 percent of his free throws, and shot over 90 percent from the line four times. Perhaps more to the point, he *always* wanted the ball when games were on the line and coming through in the clutch was almost routine for the twelve-time All-Star.

Acknowledgments

I'd like to acknowledge Niels Aaboe, senior acquisitions editor for Globe Pequot/Lyons Press, who had the idea for me to write a book that would explain the whys and wherefores of the game of football. He then had the confidence to follow that book up with this exploration of the game of basketball. Thanks also to editor Rick Rinehart for the work he contributed to this book and to production editor Jenna Dutton for helping polish the manuscript.

Thanks also to the coaches and players associated with the NBA who cooperated by granting interviews for information used in this book, especially the following: Larry Nance, John "Hot Rod" Williams, Dick Groat, Brad Daugherty, and Nate Thurmond.

Thanks also to my sons, Sean and Scott Stewart, my daughter-in law Rachel, as well as my grandson Nathan Stewart for their input and assistance in researching this book.

Finally, a note about a few of the sources I relied upon quite heavily. Without the outstanding websites of Basketball Reference, Sports Reference, NBA, Bleacher Report, Sports Illustrated, and ESPN, this book would have been much more difficult to write. Being able to explore and depend upon those sources (and others) made the book inherently more pleasurable to write.

Bibliography

Books

Aamidor, Abraham. *Chuck Taylor, All Star*. Bloomington: Indiana University Press, 2006.

Allen, Forrest C. (Phog). *Better Basketball Technique, Tactics, Tales.* Whittlesey House, 1937.

Bondy, Filip. *Who's on Worst?* New York: Doubleday, 2013.

Gergen, Joe. *The Final Four*. St. Louis: The Sporting News, 1987.

Hollander, Zander, and Alex Sachare, eds. *The Official NBA Basketball Encyclopedia*. New York: Villard Books, 1989.

MacMullan, Jackie, Rafe Bartholomew, and Dan Klores. *Basketball: A Love Story*. New York: Crown Archetype, 2018.

Shaughnessy, Dan. *Wish It Lasted Forever: Life with the Larry Bird Celtics*. New York: Scribner, 2012.

Stewart, Wayne. *The Little Giant Book of Basketball Facts*. New York: Sterling Publishing Company, Inc., 2005.

———. *You're the Basketball Ref: Mind-Boggling Questions to Test Your Basketball Knowledge*. New York: Skyhorse Publishing, 2019.

Magazines and Newspapers

Associated Press. "Hall of Famer Was One of NBA's Great Big Men." *Chronicle-Telegram,* May 12, 2022.

Cohen, Jay. "Quigley Again." Associated Press, July 9, 2022.

Martin, Bruce. "Off to the Races." *Beckett Basketball*, May 1991.

———. "Towering Twins." *Beckett Basketball*, January 1992.

Schudel, Matt. "Peter Moore, Designer of First Air Jordan Sneaker, Dies at 78." *Washington Post*, May 7, 2022.

Shaw, Mary-Liz. "Cool Runnings." *Reminisce Extra*, July 2022.

Stewart, Wayne. *Beckett Basketball Monthly*. Various issues.

White, George. "Sneaking Back: P.F. Flyers Live—This Time from Head to Toe." *Los Angeles Times*, September 15, 1988.

Websites

ajc.com

apbr.org

basketballfandom.com

basketball-reference.com

basketballnoise.com

basketballworld.com

bigbluehistory.net

bleacherreport.com

cbssports.com

celticswire.usatoday.com

cismeurope.org

clutchpoints.com

dunkorthree.com

espn.com

fadeawayworld.net

fanbuzz.com

forbes.com

forums.rivals.com

franchisesports.co.uk

harlemglobetrotters.com

hoopsgeek.com

hoopshype.com

howtheyplay.com

insidearenas.com

investopedia.com

latimes.com

landofbasketball.com

life.com

medium.com

nationalgeographic.com

nba.com

nbahoopsonline.com

nbcsports.com

ncaa.com

newarena.com

npr.org

nypost.com

proformancehoops.com

remembertheaba.com

rookieroad.com

si.com

skysports.com

sportingnews.com

sportsaday.com

sportshistorynetwork.com

sportskeeda.com

sports-reference.com

sports.yahoo.com

stadiumtalk.com

talkbasket.net

theathletic.com

therookiewire.usatoday.com

thesportsrush.com

today.com

www.vault.si.com

wbur.org

wikipedia.com

weightofstuff.com

yardbarker.com

About the Author

Wayne Stewart was born and raised in Donora, Pennsylvania, a town that has produced several big-league baseball players, including Stan Musial and the father-son Griffeys. In fact, he was on the same high school baseball team as Griffey Sr. Stewart now lives in Amherst, Ohio, with his wife, Nancy.

Covering the sports world as a writer for more than forty years, beginning in 1978, Stewart has interviewed and profiled many stars including Kareem Abdul-Jabbar, Robert Parish, Lenny Wilkens, and Larry Bird. Some of his key football interviews have taken place with legends such as Joe Montana, Raymond Berry, and Lenny Moore, and he has also interviewed numerous baseball legends such as Nolan Ryan, Bob Gibson, Tony Gwynn, Greg Maddux, Rickey Henderson, and Ken Griffey Jr.

Further, Stewart has written more than twenty-five baseball books and a handful of other books on football and basketball. His work has appeared in seven baseball anthologies. This is his thirty-ninth book.

Stewart has also written more than five hundred articles for publications such as *Baseball Digest, USA Today/Baseball Weekly, Boys' Life*, and Beckett Publications and has written for the official publications of many Major League Baseball teams including the Braves, Yankees, White Sox, Orioles, Padres, Twins, Phillies, Red Sox, A's, and Dodgers.

As well, he has appeared as a baseball expert/historian on Cleveland's Fox 8, on an ESPN Classic television show about Bob Feller, and on numerous radio shows. He has hosted his own radio shows, including a call-in sports talk show, a pregame Indians report, and pregame shows for Notre Dame football.